CAMBRIDGE
UNIVERSITY PRESS

Computer Science

for Cambridge IGCSE™ & O Level

PROGRAMMING BOOK FOR PYTHON

Chris Roffey

CAMBRIDGE
UNIVERSITY PRESS

University Printing House, Cambridge CB2 8BS, United Kingdom

One Liberty Plaza, 20th Floor, New York, NY 10006, USA

477 Williamstown Road, Port Melbourne, VIC 3207, Australia

314–321, 3rd Floor, Plot 3, Splendor Forum, Jasola District Centre, New Delhi – 110025, India

79 Anson Road, #06–04/06, Singapore 079906

Cambridge University Press is part of the University of Cambridge.

It furthers the University's mission by disseminating knowledge in the pursuit of education, learning and research at the highest international levels of excellence.

www.cambridge.org
Information on this title: www.cambridge.org/9781108951562

First published 2017
Second edition 2021

20 19 18 17 16 15 14 13 12 11 10 9 8 7 6 5 4 3 2 1

Printed in Malaysia by Vivar Printing

A catalogue record for this publication is available from the British Library

ISBN 978-1-108-95156-2 Programming Book Paperback with Digital Access (2 Years)

ISBN 978-1-108-94828-9 Digital Programming Book (2 Years)

Additional resources for this publication at www.cambridge.org/go

Cambridge University Press has no responsibility for the persistence or accuracy of URLs for external or third-party internet websites referred to in this publication, and does not guarantee that any content on such websites is, or will remain, accurate or appropriate. Information regarding prices, travel timetables, and other factual information given in this work is correct at the time of first printing but Cambridge University Press does not guarantee the accuracy of such information thereafter.

Third-party websites and resources referred to in this publication have not been endorsed by Cambridge Assessment International Education.

Exam-style questions and sample answers have been written by the authors. In examinations, the way marks are awarded may be different. References to assessment and/or assessment preparation are the publisher's interpretation of the syllabus requirements and may not fully reflect the approach of Cambridge Assessment International Education.

The information in Chapter 14 is based on the Cambridge IGCSE, IGCSE (9-1) and O Level Computer Science syllabuses (0478/0984/2210) for examination from 2023. You should always refer to the appropriate syllabus document for the year of your examination to confirm the details and for more information. The syllabus documents are available on the Cambridge International website at *www.cambridgeinternational.org*

DEDICATED TEACHER AWARDS

Teachers play an important part in shaping futures. Our Dedicated Teacher Awards recognise the hard work that teachers put in every day.

Thank you to everyone who nominated this year; we have been inspired and moved by all of your stories. Well done to all of our nominees for your dedication to learning and for inspiring the next generation of thinkers, leaders and innovators.

Congratulations to our incredible winner and finalists!

WINNER

Patricia Abril	Stanley Manaay	Tiffany Cavanagh	Helen Comerford	John Nicko Coyoca	Meera Rangarajan
New Cambridge School, Colombia	Salvacion National High School, Philippines	Trident College Solwezi, Zambia	Lumen Christi Catholic College, Australia	University of San Jose-Recoletos, Philippines	RBK International Academy, India

For more information about our dedicated teachers and their stories, go to
dedicatedteacher.cambridge.org

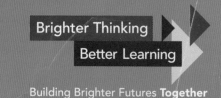

Building Brighter Futures **Together**

> Contents

The items in orange are available on the digital edition that accompanies this book.

> Introduction

This fully revised edition reflects the new Cambridge IGCSE™, IGCSE (9–1) and O Level Computer Science syllabuses (0478/0984/2210). It includes all new tasks and challenges based on feedback from readers and teachers. But the aim of this edition remains true to the original: to provide a programming book that specifically covers the material relevant to the syllabuses. This book will also provide you with a starting point in the exciting and rewarding process of being able to create your own computer programs. I hope you find the book a helpful step into the world of computer science.

Language

The syntax and structures used to implement programming techniques vary across different languages. This book is entirely based around Python 3, one of the three recommended languages for the syllabuses. Similar books are also available which focus on Microsoft® Visual Basic and Java programming languages.

Python has, at its core, the principle that code should be easy to read. This means that in many ways it is very close to pseudocode. The pseudocode structure used in the examination papers uses a language-neutral style. You will need to become familiar with this, and be able to read and follow the logic easily. When writing your own pseudocode the most important thing is to ensure your logic is clear. Pseudocode is meant to be a way of expressing clearly the logic of a program, free from the worries of syntax.

Python also has a recommended style guide that can be found at the python.org website. Here, for example, it is recommended that Python programmers name functions and variables with descriptive all lower case characters separated by underscores, for example, `my_variable`. As it could be very confusing to keep swapping naming conventions, this book assumes that you are going to stick, wherever possible, to the correct Python style but be a flexible enough thinker to be able to read other pseudocode styles. It is recommended that when preparing for examinations, you ensure you are aware of the exam board variable naming style.

Support

As you work your way through the exercises in this book you will develop your computational thinking skills, independent of any specific programming language. You will do this through the use of program design tools such as structure diagrams and flowcharts. You will also make use of pseudocode, a structured method for describing the logic of computer programs.

It is crucial that you become familiar with these techniques. Throughout this book, all the programming techniques are demonstrated in the non-language-specific format required, with the exception of variable and function naming.

To support learning, many of the chapters include exam-style tasks. Solutions to all the chapter tasks can be found on the digital part of this resource. There are examples of appropriate solutions that show how to turn logical ideas into actual programs. There is also a series of exam-style questions in Chapter 15.

Developing programming skills

One of the advantages of Python is that it provides a language that encourages you to program solutions making use of the basic programming constructs: sequence, selection and iteration. Although the language does have access to many powerful pre-written code libraries, they are not generally used in this book.

Computational thinking is the ability to break down a problem into its constituent parts and to provide a logical and efficient coded solution. Experience shows that knowing how to think computationally relies much more on an understanding of the underlying programming concepts than on the ability to learn a few shortcut library routines.

This book is aimed at teaching those underlying skills which can be applied to the languages of the future. It is without doubt that programming languages will develop over the coming years, but the ability to think computationally will remain a constant. As technology increasingly impacts on society, people with computation thinking skills will be able to help shape the way that technology impacts on our future.

> How to use this book

Throughout this book, you will notice lots of different features that will help your learning. These are explained below.

LEARNING INTENTIONS

These set the scene for each chapter, help with navigation through the Python programming process and indicate the important concepts in each topic.

SKILLS FOCUS

This feature supports your computational thinking, mathematical and programming skills. They include useful explanations, step-by-step examples and questions for you to try out yourselves.

KEY WORDS

Key vocabulary is highlighted in the text when it is first introduced. Definitions are then given in the margin, which explain the meanings of these words and phrases. You will also find definitions of these words in the glossary at the back of this book.

Pseudocode and Code snippets

Python code is presented with syntax highlighting in the same way that IDEs present different programming terms in different colours.

```python
number1 = int(input('Enter first number: '))
number2 = int(input('Enter second number: '))
if number2 == number1:
    print('Same')
else:
    if number2 > number1:
        print('Second')
    else:
        print('First')
```

Code snippet 7.3

Pseudocode is shown in text like this:

```
INPUT number1
INPUT number2
answer ← number1 + number2
OUTPUT answer
```

Code snippet 3.1

TIPS

These are short suggestions to remind you about important learning points. For example, a tip to help clear up misunderstandings between pseudocode and Python.

Further Information: This feature highlights the advanced aspects in this book that go beyond the immediate scope of the syllabuses.

Programming tasks

Programming tasks give you the opportunity to develop your programming and problem-solving skills. Answers to these questions can be found in the solutions chapter, on the digital part of this resource. There are three different types of programming tasks:

DEMO TASKS

You will be presented with a task and a step-by-step solution will be provided to help familiarise you with the techniques required.

PRACTICE TASKS

Questions provide opportunities for developing skills that you have learnt about in the demo tasks.

CHALLENGE TASKS

Challenge tasks will stretch and challenge you even further.

INTERACTIVE SESSION

Interactive sessions are used to illustrate simple concepts or to show the correct use of some new syntax. You can copy these directly into your online Python environment to follow along with the book. You may then want to experiment further to deepen your understanding.

SUMMARY

There is a summary of key points at the end of each chapter.

END-OF-CHAPTER TASKS

Questions at the end of each chapter provide more demanding programming tasks, some of which may require use of knowledge from previous chapters. Answers to these questions can be found in the solutions chapter, on the digital part of this resource.

NOTE: As there are some differences in the way programming statements are structured between languages, you should always refer back to the syllabus pseudocode guide to see how algorithms will be presented in your exam.

> How to use this series

The coursebook provides coverage of the full Cambridge IGCSE, IGCSE (9–1) and O Level Computer Science syllabuses (0478/0984/2210) for first examination from 2023. Each chapter explains facts and concepts and uses relevant real-world contexts to bring topics to life, including two case studies from Microsoft® Research. There is a skills focus feature containing worked examples and questions to develop learners' mathematical, computational thinking and programming skills, as well as a programming tasks feature to build learners' problem-solving skills. The programming tasks include 'getting started' skills development questions and 'challenge' tasks to ensure support is provided for every learner. Questions and exam-style questions in every chapter help learners to consolidate their understanding.

The digital teacher's resource contains detailed guidance for all topics of the syllabuses, including common misconceptions to elicit the areas where learners might need extra support, as well as an engaging bank of lesson ideas for each syllabus topic. Differentiation is emphasised with advice for identification of different learner needs and suggestions of appropriate interventions to support and stretch learners.

The digital teacher's resource also contains scaffolded worksheets for each chapter, as well as practice exam-style papers. Answers are freely accessible to teachers on the 'supporting resources' area of the Cambridge GO platform.

There are three programming books: one for each of the recommended languages in the syllabuses – Python, Microsoft Visual Basic and Java. Each of the books are made up of programming tasks that follow a scaffolded approach to skills development. This allows learners to gradually progress through 'demo', 'practice' and 'challenge' tasks to ensure that every learner is supported. There is also a chapter dedicated to programming scenario tasks to provide support for this area of the syllabuses. The digital part of each book contains a comprehensive solutions chapter, giving step-by-step answers to the tasks in the book.

> Chapter 1
Python 3

IN THIS CHAPTER YOU WILL:

- obtain a simple Interactive Development Environment (IDE) to support your programming
- use both interactive mode and script mode in Python
- program and save a text-based application in script mode
- learn how to use the built-in turtle module.

Introduction

Python is a modern, powerful programming language used by many organisations such as YouTube, Wikipedia, Google, Dropbox, CERN and NASA. At the time of writing, Python is listed as the third most popular programming language in the world.

Python 3 is the latest version of the Python programming language. It is a loosely typed script language. **Loosely typed** means that it is usually not necessary to declare variable types; the interpreter looks after this. A compiler converts instructions into machine code that can be read and executed by a computer. Script languages do not have a compiler. This means that, in general, Python programs cannot run as quickly as compiled languages. However, this brings numerous advantages such as fast and agile development.

> **KEY WORD**
>
> **loosely typed:** programming languages, such as Python, where the programmer does not have to declare the variable type when initialising or declaring variables.

1.1 Getting Python 3 and IDLE

There are Python 3 installers for most types of computer available on the python.org website. You should choose the latest stable version of Python 3 (Python 3.8.1 at time of writing). When downloaded and installed, you will find Python comes with a perfectly good IDE called IDLE. Starting up IDLE will enable you to run a program straight away.

An **Integrated Development Environment (IDE)** is a piece of software that is similar to a word processor but for writing programs. IDEs provide special tools that help programmers do their jobs more efficiently. They usually have an easy way of running the programs during the development stage – such as a Run button. There are many IDEs that can be used with Python. Some of them are very complicated to use, with many specialist tools for teams of developers that work on very large projects. **IDLE** is an IDE that has all the tools a learner requires and very little to get in your way. Everything that you are asked to do in this book can be done with IDLE. Figure 1.1 shows what you are presented with when you first open IDLE.

> **KEY WORDS**
>
> **Integrated Development Environment (IDE):** software that helps programmers to design, create and test program code.
>
> **IDLE:** the IDE provided when Python is installed.

```
● ● ●                        Python 3.8.1 Shell
Python 3.8.1 (v3.8.1:1b293b6006, Dec 18 2019, 14:08:53)
[Clang 6.0 (clang-600.0.57)] on darwin
Type "help", "copyright", "credits" or "license()" for more information.
>>>



                                                      Ln: 4   Col: 4
```

Figure 1.1: IDLE's Python shell on an Apple computer

Figure 1.1 shows the **Python shell**, which is the first thing that opens when you start IDLE. This is an unusual feature in Python. In the shell, we can write Python commands and code snippets and run them without having to save a file. In this book, we will refer to typing code into the shell as an 'interactive session'. Interactive sessions are great for experimenting and trying out new things that you learn about Python. When you are presented with an interactive session, it is expected that you will open a Python shell and type in what is shown. When you have done this, you are encouraged to then try out your own ideas until you feel confident with the new feature. Open IDLE from your Python install folder now and follow the instructions in the interactive session below.

INTERACTIVE SESSION

Open a Python shell and type in the following code after the >>> prompt:

```
>>> print('Hello world!')
```

Press return.

You have now run your first **interactive mode** program. Your code told the computer to print the text 'Hello world!' to the screen. It **executed** your code when you pressed the return key on your keyboard. You can also use interactive mode as a simple calculator. Try entering this sum and press return:

```
>>> 3*4
```

TIP

Interactive sessions are used to illustrate simple concepts or to show the correct use of some new syntax. It is a good idea to start your own interactive session and follow along with the book. You may then want to experiment further to deepen your understanding.

Sometimes we want to save our programs; this is not possible in the Python shell. To do this we open a file, type in our code and then save the file with a .py extension. In this book, we refer to this as working in **script mode**. In Python we can have the Python shell open at the same time as a script window. This means that while writing a program, you can still swap into the Python shell to try out something before continuing to write your program.

The Python shell serves another purpose. It is where you can type any input a program asks for and it is where any output appears. In IDLE the two windows are separate and you are free to arrange your desktop as you wish. To open a new file for programming in script mode you click on *File* and then *New File* as shown in Figure 1.2 on the following page.

Python shell: a window that allows Python programmers to write and run code a line at a time without having to save the code in a file. It is also where users can provide input and where output is sent.

interactive mode: when writing and running code in the Python shell window, interactive mode allows us to try out snippets of code without saving.

execute: another word for run. Programmers tend to prefer to talk about a program executing rather than running, but they mean the same thing.

script mode: Python scripts are written in a text editor or IDE and saved with the .py extension. Script mode enables programmers to write longer programs that can be edited or run at any time in the future.

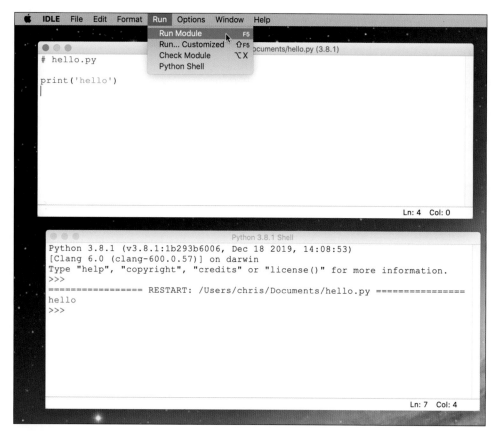

Figure 1.2: IDLE open on an Apple computer

In the top window in Figure 1.2, you can see that a very small program has been written and then saved with the name hello.py. Once the file is saved, the program can be run by choosing *Run Module* from the *Run* menu. Notice how the output appears in the Python shell window underneath.

PRACTICE TASK 1.1

Hello world

Using IDLE in script mode, open a new file and write the following program:

```
# hello.py
print('Hello world!')
```

Then, save it to your Documents folder and run your program by selecting *Run Module* from the *Run* menu or pressing F5 on your keyboard.

1.2 Other Integrated Development Environments (IDEs)

As mentioned in Section 1.1, there are many other IDEs available. If you have a Raspberry Pi, Python is already installed and so is another IDE called Thonny. This again is a relatively simple tool that is similar to IDLE. Thonny has some extra features to help learners understand what is happening in their more complicated programs.

On the Raspberry Pi, you can start Thonny by selecting *Thonny Python IDE* from *Programming* in the main *Menu* in the task bar (Figure 1.3).

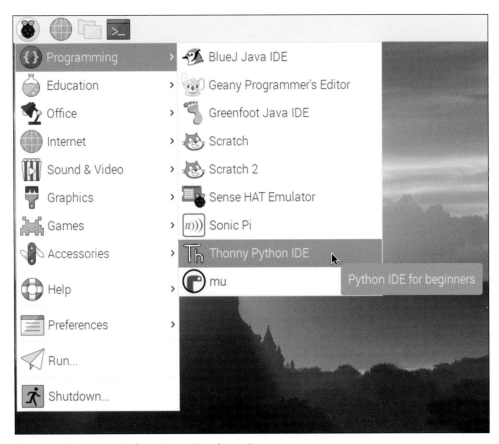

Figure 1.3: Starting Python 3 on a Raspberry Pi

This opens Thonny, which contains both a Python shell and a script area in a single window, as shown in Figure 1.4.

Figure 1.4: Thonny on a Raspberry Pi; the script area is on the top and the Python shell underneath

You can carry out interactive sessions by typing directly into Thonny's Python shell area. Script mode is started by selecting *New* from the *File* menu. Thonny is available for all major computers, not just the Raspberry Pi.

IDLE and Thonny are perfectly adequate for performing all the tasks required in this book. However, if you have been programming with IDLE for a little while, you might like to try one of the many other IDEs available.

The one that is used for the remainder of the screenshots in this chapter, and occasionally later in the book, is Wing IDE 101 (Figure 1.5). This is a free version of a commercial IDE that provides a carefully selected set of facilities that are useful for students. It can be downloaded from the Wingware website, where brief introductory videos and installation instructions are also available. Wing IDE 101 is available for Windows, Apple and Linux computers.

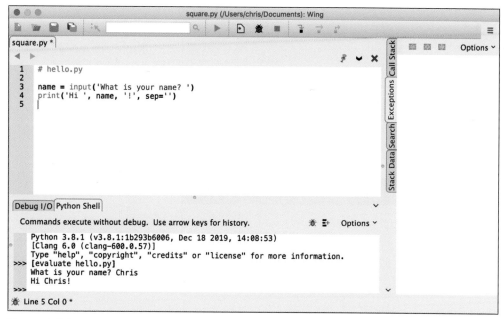

Figure 1.5: Wing IDE 101 Integrated Development Environment

The large panel in the middle of the application is where you write your scripts. Interactive sessions can be run in the Python shell tab below this window.

There are two ways to run a program in Wing IDE. Clicking the run button ▶ will access the Python shell as shown in Figure 1.5. An alternative – and recommended – way of running your scripts is to click on the bug 🐞 to the right of the run button (Figure 1.6). This opens the Debug I/O panel and now provides error messages in the Exceptions tab on the right.

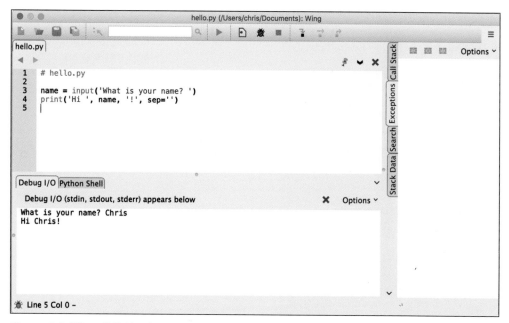

Figure 1.6: Wing IDE 101 showing input and output after pressing the bug button

PRACTICE TASK 1.2

Input and output

Using your chosen IDE in script mode, open a new file and write, save and run the hello.py program shown in Figure 1.6. Note that when it is running, the program will print out 'What is your name?' in the Python shell. The program will then wait for you to type in your name and press the return key on your keyboard before finishing.

CHALLENGE TASK 1.1

Two inputs and an output

Using your chosen IDE in script mode, open a new file and write, save and run a program that asks users for their first name and then their last name. It should then output a greeting that includes their full name.

TIP

There are many excellent IDEs available to choose from but, if you are new to programming, you will not go wrong choosing IDLE, Thonny or Wing IDE 101.

1.3 Turtle graphics

Python has a special **built-in** module that we can use to create programs that draw patterns. This is an implementation of the turtle graphics part of the Logo programming language. The great thing about this module is that the simple turtle commands can be combined with Python code. This means that, as we learn more about Python, we will be able to make more sophisticated and interesting turtle programs. Many of the chapters in this book will have one or two turtle tasks for you to try.

A turtle is a robot (see Figure 1.7) that can be programmed to draw a line by following a path and placing a pen on the floor to create a line.

KEY WORD

built-in: when programming, we can write our own commands. Python comes with some ready-made commands and modules. The `print()` function is a built-in function and turtle is an example of a built-in module.

Figure 1.7: A floor turtle

The language that is used to control the robot consists of simple directional commands and is based on the Logo programming language. There are many online sites and applications that allow users to control an onscreen turtle by using the Logo programming language. The language and syntax have developed a long way from the early Logo language. Some modern implementations provide multiple turtles and complex 3D graphics.

A few commands for a floor turtle are shown in Table 1.1:

| Turtle command | Meaning |
	distances in pixels (1 cm ≈ 20 pixels)
forward(d)	Move d pixels forwards
backward(d)	Move d pixels backwards
left(t)	Turn left t degrees
right(t)	Turn right t degrees
penup()	Raise the pen (stop drawing)
pendown()	Lower the pen (start drawing)

Table 1.1: Commands for a floor turtle

Using just these few commands, we can create simple line drawings on our computer screen.

DEMO TASK 1.1

Draw a square

Using Python's turtle module, write a program that draws a square.

Solution

First write a line of code (line 3 in Figure 1.8) that imports the turtle module into our program. This gives us access to the turtle commands. Then write some turtle commands that draw a square. You can see the complete program in Figure 1.8.

```
# square.py - /Users/chris/Documents/square.py (3.8.1)*
1 # square.py
2
3 from turtle import *
4
5 forward(100)
6 right(90)
7 forward(100)
8 right(90)
9 forward(100)
10 right(90)
11 forward(100)|
                                    Ln: 11   Col: 12
```

Figure 1.8: A turtle program written in script mode using IDLE

CONTINUED

This program will work well in IDLE and Thonny. However, in Wing IDE 101, the window with the square in will disappear as soon as the program has finished. In Wing IDE, two more lines of code are required: we need to import another module (see line 4 in Figure 1.9) and then add another line of code to keep the window that contains the 'turtle' open (see line 14 in Figure 1.9).

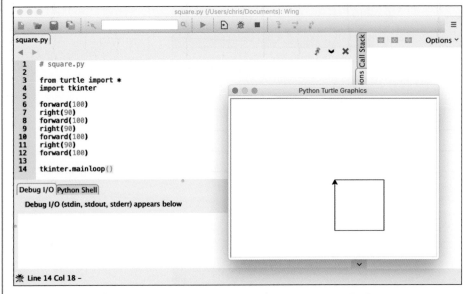

Figure 1.9: A turtle program written in script mode using Wing IDE 101

PRACTICE TASK 1.3

Draw a square

Open your preferred IDE and write, save and run the square.py program shown in Figure 1.8 and Figure 1.9.

CHALLENGE TASK 1.2

Draw a triangle

Open your preferred IDE and write, save and run a turtle program that draws an equilateral triangle.

SKILLS FOCUS 1.1

Python 3 is an industry standard programming language. It comes with many commands that are ready to use – for example, print() and input(). However, there is also a large library of other commands we can use if we import one of the many built-in modules that come with the standard install. Two modules that you have already seen in this chapter are the turtle and **tkinter** modules.

KEY WORD

tkinter: a module that is provided as part of the standard library in Python. It provides tools to help the programmer build applications that have buttons, textboxes, etc.

CONTINUED

There are different ways of importing these modules. How you import them affects the way you have to write your commands. In Figure 1.9, you can see two different ways of importing these modules on lines 3 and 4. In line 3, the turtle module is imported with the following line of code:

```
from turtle import *
```

When you realise that * stands for everything, the line of code makes sense. It means, 'import every command available in the turtle module'. As long as we know what the commands are, doing things this way means we can then use all of the turtle commands in a straightforward way (as illustrated in Figure 1.9, lines 6 to 12).

Syntax is the term used to refer to a program's grammar. The syntax used on line 4, in Figure 1.9, shows another way to import a module:

```
import tkinter
```

The tkinter module gives us access to a lot of graphical programming tools, but what is important here is how, when importing a module with this syntax, we have to use different syntax to call the turtle commands. When we import tkinter like this, we have to precede the tkinter commands with the name of the module and a dot like this:

```
tkinter.mainloop()
```

Question

1 Rewrite lines 6–12 from Figure 1.9 so that the program will run correctly when we import turtle with import turtle.

You may be wondering why we would ever do this because it results in far more typing for the programmer. In larger programs, there may be several modules imported. It can then become confusing which commands are from the standard library and which are from the various modules. This becomes much clearer when they are all preceded by the module's name. Also, because the programmer might not know the complete set of commands available in a module, they might name one of their own commands with a name that is available in the module. This would cause their program to fail to run.

There is another way of importing a module that is a kind of compromise between the previous two systems. Study the following program to see how this third system works:

```
import turtle as t
t.forward(100)
t.right(90)
t.forward(100)
t.right(90)
t.forward(100)
t.right(90)
t.forward(100)
```

Code snippet 1.1

TIP

It is considered good practice, when importing more than one module, to only import one module with the from <module> import * syntax. This is what we did in the program shown in Figure 1.9.

CONTINUED

For the most part, in this book, we are going to use the original form of import (`from turtle import *`) where we can just type the commands from the turtle module on their own. Nevertheless, it is important to understand that there are other ways of importing modules for when you start to read other people's programs.

There are more turtle commands available than those shown in Table 1.1. To help you answer the turtle tasks that are found in later chapters, there is a list of the most useful turtle commands in Appendix 1 at the end of the book. You may wish to have a look now and experiment with what you can do with turtle.

1.4 Graphical user interface (GUI) applications

Note: GUI applications are optional. They are not covered in the syllabuses.

Although not required by the syllabuses, your Python scripts are not limited to text-based applications. By importing the tkinter module, it is easy to produce visually rich **graphical user interfaces (GUIs)** and attach your **algorithms** to buttons in windows.

Chapter 5, GUI applications, is an optional chapter included in this book. In it, you will learn how to build your own GUIs and how to repurpose your algorithm solutions to work with them. From Chapter 5 onwards, there will be some tasks provided that include making GUIs. Although these are not required by the syllabuses, repurposing your solutions to work with GUIs will make you a more flexible programmer and allow you to produce more professional looking applications.

1.5 Additional support

The intention of this book is to introduce programming concepts that make use of the non-language-specific formats included in the syllabuses. Python 3 provides you with the opportunity to use a real programming language to develop your understanding of these concepts. The official documentation for the Python programming language can be accessed through the python.org website.

A simple syntax reference guide that can be printed out and fits in your pocket is available from the Coding Club website. You can find the link to the website in the digital part of the book.

KEY WORDS

graphical user interface (GUI): an interface that includes graphical elements, such as windows, icons and buttons.

algorithm: a process, instructions or set of rules to be followed during the execution of a program.

SUMMARY

Python 3 is a loosely typed programming language that is designed to encourage easily read code.
Python 3 comes with a simple Integrated Development Environment called IDLE.
There are many other IDEs available, such as Thonny and Wing IDE 101, both of which are specifically designed for students.
There are three main styles of programming in Python 3: • interactive mode: quick tests and trials that can be programmed in the Python shell • script mode: text-based scripts that can be saved so that your applications can be reused • GUI applications: full, visually rich applications that can be produced in script mode.
As well as the basic programming commands available in Python, there is a large library of specialist modules that come with Python and can be imported into your programs such as the turtle and tkinter modules.

END-OF-CHAPTER TASKS

1   In your preferred IDE, write a text-based program that asks users to input their age and then their name.
    Your program should then output a phrase similar to: 'Hi Vipul. You are 16.'

2   Write a turtle program that draws the house shown here:

> **TIP**
>
> Don't forget the main turtle commands are all listed in Appendix 1 at the end of the book.

3   Write a turtle program that draws a regular pentagon with sides of length 100 pixels.

› Chapter 2
Variables and arithmetic operators

IN THIS CHAPTER YOU WILL:

- declare and use variables and constants

- use the data types Integer, Real, Char, String and Boolean

- use basic mathematical operators to process input values

- design and represent simple programs using flowcharts and pseudocode

- write simple Python programs that can be run and debugged

- learn how to generate random numbers and round decimals.

Introduction

Programs need to store information. This information is stored in variables. The information stored can be numbers, for example, the cost of an item in an online store or the experience points gained by a character in a video game. However, the information could just as easily be some text, such as the name of a person or item. The values stored in variables may need to be updated as a program is run or used to calculate new data. To do this you can use simple mathematical operators. You will be familiar with most of the mathematical operators, such as addition and subtraction, from your maths lessons. This chapter explains how to use variables and mathematical operators when designing and writing Python programs.

2.1 Variables and constants

Programs are normally designed to accept and input data. They also process the data to produce the required output. There are different data types: a calculator will process numerical data; a program that checks email addresses will process text data. When writing programs, you will use variables or constants to refer to these data values. A **variable** identifies data that can be changed during the execution of a program. A **constant** is used for data values that remain fixed. In many computer languages, the **data type** must be provided when **declaring** or **initialising variables**. The data type is used by the computer to allocate a suitable location in memory. These languages, such as Java, are said to be strongly typed.

Python is an example of a loosely typed programming language. The computer decides on a variable's data type from the context you provide. Compare these two variable declarations, first in Visual Basic then in Python.

In Visual Basic:

```
Dim Score As Integer = 0
```

In Python:

```
score = 0
```

The same declaration, in pseudocode:

```
Score ← 0
```

Although loosely typed languages are easy for the programmer to write, it is still important to be aware what data type your variables contain.

2.2 Types of data

How can we know what data type has been allocated by Python in our programs? To find out the data type of a variable or constant being used in a Python program, use the built-in `type()` function. Study this interactive session in the Python shell to see how to use this function:

KEY WORDS

variable: a memory location used to store a value; the value of the data can be changed during program execution.

constant: a named memory location used to store a value; the value can be used but not changed during program execution. (However, in Python, we use normal variables but indicate that the value of the data should not be changed by giving it a name in all capitals, e.g. PI = 3.14).

data type: a specification of the kind of value that a variable will store.

declaring variables: setting up a variable or constant. It is important to declare or initialise global variables.

initialising variables: giving a variable a start (initial) value when it is first declared.

INTERACTIVE SESSION

```
>>> my_integer = 3
>>> type(my_integer)
<class 'int'>
>>> my_string = 'hello'
>>> type(my_string)
<class 'str'>
```

The most important data types you need to know are shown in Table 2.1:

Data type	Description and Use	Python type(variable) query returns:
Integer	Whole numbers, either positive or negative. Used with quantities such as the number of students at a school – you cannot have half a student.	`'int'`
Real	Positive or negative fractional values. Used with numerical values that require decimal parts, such as currency. Real is the data type used by many programming languages and is also referred to in the syllabuses.	`'float'` Python does not use the term Real. The equivalent data type in Python is called `'floating point'`.

Char	A single character or symbol (for example, A, z, $, 6).
	
	A Char variable that holds a digit; it cannot be used in calculations.
		`'str'`
		
		Python treats characters as small strings.
		
		Note:
		
		```>>> my_var = '3'```
		```>>> type(my_var)```
		```<class 'str'>```
		```>>> my_var = 3```
		```>>> type(my_var)```
		```<class 'int'>```

String	More than one character (a string of characters).
	
	Used to hold words, names or sentences but also punctuation, numbers as text, etc.
		`'str'`
		
		e.g.
		
		```>>> my_string = 'yellow'```
		```>>> type(my_var)```
		```<class 'str'>```
		```>>> mobile = '0774 333 333'```
		```>>> type(my_var)```
		```<class 'str'>```

Boolean	One of two values, either TRUE or FALSE.
	
	Used to indicate the result of a condition. For example, in a computer game, a Boolean variable might be used to store whether a player has chosen to have the sound effects on.
		`'bool'`
		
		e.g.
		
		```>>> sfx = False```
		```>>> type(sfx)```
		```<class 'bool'>```

Table 2.1: Data types

2.3 Pseudo numbers

Telephone numbers and ISBN numbers are not really numbers. They are a collection of digits used to uniquely identify an item. Sometimes they contain spaces or start with a zero. They are not intended to be used in calculations. These are known as pseudo numbers and it is normal to store them in a String variable. If you store a mobile phone number as an integer, any leading zeroes will be removed, while spaces and symbols are not permitted.

2.4 Naming conventions in Python

There are a variety of naming conventions in Python. Here are a few of them.

Variable names

Use all lower case, starting with a letter and joining words with underscores. It is considered good practice to use descriptive names. This aids readability and reduces the need for so much commenting. **Commenting** is where the programmer writes notes in the program that the computer ignores. In Python these start with the # symbol. In pseudocode, comments are preceded with two slashes (//). You can see examples of commented code in Demo Task 2.1 in Section 2.6, later in this chapter.

For example:

```
score_total = 56    ✓
Total = 56          ✗
t = 56              ✗
```

> **Further Information:**
>
> There are 31 reserved words that have a defined function in the Python programming language. These words cannot be used as your own variable names:
>
> and as assert break class continue def del elif else except finally for from global if import in is lambda nonlocal not or pass print raise return try while with yield.

> **KEY WORD**
>
> **commenting:** adding human readable notes to a program. The comments are intended to help explain how the code works. Comments are ignored by the computer when the code is executed. In pseudocode, comments are preceded with two forward slashes // and in Python by a hash symbol #.

Constants

Constants are values that do not vary. Constants keep the same value throughout our programs. Use all upper case characters to indicate constants.

In Python:

```
PI = 3.1415
```

In pseudocode:

```
CONSTANT PI ← 3.1415
```

2.5 Arithmetic operators

There are a number of operations that can be performed on numerical data in your programs.

The most important operators used in Python 3 and their equivalent in pseudocode are shown in Table 2.2:

Operation	Example of use	Description

Addition	Python:
	
	`result = num1 + num2`
	
	Pseudocode:
	
	`result ← num1 + num2`
		Adds the values held in the variables `num1` and `num2` and stores the result in the variable `result`.

Subtraction	Python:
	
	`result = num1 - num2`
	
	Pseudocode:
	
	`result ← num1 - num2`
		Subtracts the value held in `num2` from the value in `num1` and stores the result in the variable `result`.

Multiplication	Python:
	
	`result = num1 * num2`
	
	Pseudocode:
	
	`result ← num1 * num2`
		Multiplies the values held in the variables `num1` and `num2` and stores the result in the variable `result`.

Power of	Python:
	
	`result = num1 ** num2`
	
	Pseudocode:
	
	`result ← num1 ^ num2`
		Raises the value held in `num1` to the power of `num2`. e.g. `result = 3 ** 2` is the Python version of 3^2 and is written `3 ^ 2` in pseudocode.

Division	Python:
	
	`result = num1 / num2`
	
	Pseudocode:
	
	`result ← num1 / num2`
		Divides the value held in the variable `num1` by the value held in `num2` and stores the result in the variable `result`.

Integer Division	Python:
	
	`result = num1 // num2`
	
	Pseudocode:
	
	`result ← num1 DIV num2`
		Finds the number of times `num2` can go into `num1` completely, discards the remainder, and stores the result in the variable `result`.

(continued)

Operation	Example of use	Description

Modulus	**Python:**
	
	`result = num1 % num2`
	
	Pseudocode:
	
	`result ← num1 MOD num2`
		Finds the number of times num2 can go into num1 completely, discards this value, and stores the remainder in the variable `result`.

Table 2.2: Operators used in Python 3 and pseudocode

TIP

In your maths lessons you may have been taught the acronym BIDMAS (sometimes BODMAS or BOMDAS). The order of mathematical operations in programming languages is the same as that taught in maths lessons.

e.g. 3 × 4 + 7 ÷ 4 = 13.75

However, this is very difficult to read and many errors can creep into programs if we rely on doing this correctly. This is why programmers prefer to use plenty of brackets, and you should too.

e.g.

```
>>> (3*4) + (7/4)
13.75
```

INTERACTIVE SESSION

Now is a good time to open up a Python shell and have an interactive session to try out some of these operators yourself. To get you started, try entering the code shown below into the Python shell, pressing return after each line.

```
>>> a = 7
>>> b = 3
>>> c = a/b
>>> type(c)
>>> print(c)
```

PRACTICE TASK 2.1

Data type

Find out what value is stored in c after completing the interactive session.

2.6 Programming tasks

DEMO TASK 2.1

Multiply machine

Produce a program called 'Multiply machine' that takes two numbers input by the user. It then multiplies them together and outputs the result.

Solution

For this demo task, first we need to design the algorithm. Flowchart 2.1 shows one solution and Code snippet 2.1 shows a pseudocode solution. The next chapter will explain how you can make your own flowcharts and write your own pseudocode.

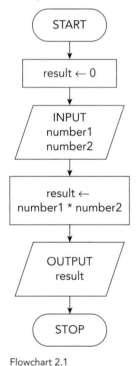

Flowchart 2.1

```
result ← 0

INPUT number1
INPUT number2

result ← number1 * number2

OUTPUT result
```
Code snippet 2.1

> **TIP**
>
> Whenever you are provided with a programming demo task, it is a good idea to open a new file in script mode and copy in the code provided. Think about what each line of code is doing as you type. Then save the script and try it out.

CONTINUED

In Python, assignment is indicated by the use of the = symbol.
In pseudocode, the ← is used.

TIP

We need to use Python's `input()` function to send a message to the user and collect their keyboard input. You will find you need to remember that `input()` only returns string data types, so if we need to do calculations on numbers supplied by the user, we will have to **cast** the string into an integer by using the `int()` function.

For example.:

```
age = int(input('How old are you?'))
```

KEY WORD

cast: the process of changing the data type of a given variable into another data type. For example, a variable that holds the string value '2' could be cast into an integer variable storing the value 2.

Here is a Python implementation of the solution shown in Flowchart 2.1 and the pseudocode:

```
# multiply_demo.py

# Initialise a variable to keep track of the result
result = 0

# Request and store user input
number1 = int(input('Please insert first number: '))
number2 = int(input('Please insert second number: '))

result = number1 * number2

# Display the value held in the variable result
print('The answer is ', result)

# End nicely by waiting for the user to press the return key.
input('\n\nPress RETURN to finish.')
```

Code snippet 2.2

It is worth noting that initialisation of `result` is not necessary in this program. It is used here to illustrate the initialisation process.

PRACTICE TASK 2.2

Remainder machine

Produce a program called 'Remainder machine' that takes two numbers input by the user. It then outputs the remainder after dividing the first number by the second.

CHALLENGE TASKS 2.1–2.2

2.1 Volume of a sphere

Design a program where the input is the diameter of a sphere (in metres) and the output is the volume of the sphere (in cubic metres). The formula you will need is $V = 4/3 * \pi * r^3$.

2.2 Grass seed calculator

A gardener sows grass seed at $50\,g/m^2$. She works for many people in a week. She wants a calculator where she can estimate lawns as rectangles and find out how much grass seed is required. Write a program that takes the length and width of a lawn in metres and outputs the amount of grass seed required in grams.

2.7 Python modules

You may recall from earlier in the chapter that there are 31 reserved words in Python that you cannot use as identifiers in your programs. This only applies when using the core features of the language. Python also has lots of libraries of other code you can use in your programs. These are called modules. There are many built-in modules. There are also many more that have been made by other programmers around the world that you can use and, of course, you can make your own.

In the end-of-chapter tasks, we are going to use two built-in modules: `random` and `turtle`. In Chapter 5, we will introduce another built-in module that will enable you to add a GUI to your programs. To access the tools in these modules, we first have to import them. A complex program might import several different modules. This means that we are considerably increasing the number of reserved words that we cannot use as our own identifiers. It is tempting to import everything in a module with code like this:

```
from turtle import *  // import everything from the turtle library
```

Now we can easily create a window with a 'turtle' in it that moves forwards and draws a line of length 100 pixels with one line of code:

```
forward(100)
```

Figure 2.1 shows how this appears on screen.

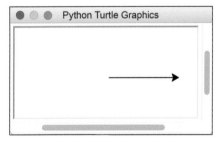

Figure 2.1: A window with a 'turtle' that has moved forwards 100 pixels

However, there are now lots of new words we have to be careful about using in our programs. It is safer to import your modules in the following way:

```
import turtle
```

This still gives your programs access to all the tools in this module but it now requires you to add `turtle.` to all your commands. For example, to move the turtle forwards, we now need to write:

```
turtle.forward(100)
```

By importing modules in this way, we no longer need to worry about confusing keywords from the turtle module with words we choose to use as identifiers elsewhere in our programs. Equally important, it is now very clear where the `forward()` command is coming from.

As you become more experienced, you will meet many programs that import modules in a variety of ways. Generally speaking, if your programs import only one module, it is usually fine to use the `from turtle import *` syntax and save yourself the extra typing.

PRACTICE TASK 2.3

Drawing squares

Write a program that inputs the side-length of a square (in pixels). As output, the turtle should draw a square on the screen with the required dimensions.

For this task you need to import Python's turtle module in the first line of your program like this:

```
from turtle import *
```

To move the turtle forwards, drawing a line behind it, use this code:

```
forward(d)
```

where d is the distance in pixels you want to move.

To turn the turtle to the right, use this code:

```
right(a)
```

where a is the angle in degrees you want to turn.

CHALLENGE TASK 2.3

Drawing hexagons

Write a program that inputs the side-length of a hexagon (in pixels). As output, the turtle should draw a regular hexagon on the screen with the required dimensions.

2.8 Random and Round

It is easy to generate a random number when we require one in our programs. In pseudocode, or in a flowchart, this is achieved by calling RANDOM(). This generates a random decimal number between 0 and 1. We can assign it to a variable in the usual way:

```
my_random_number ← RANDOM()
```

This may not be what we want though. For example, we may want a random integer from 1 to 10. This can be achieved by combining RANDOM() with ROUND(). ROUND() takes two arguments: the identifier of the number we want to be rounded, and the number of decimal places to round to (0 = integers). Putting these two functions together we can write:

```
my_dice_role ← ROUND(RANDOM()*10, 0)
```

The corresponding random function works differently in Python. First we need to import the random module at the start of our program and then call the randint() function. randint() returns a random integer. It takes two integers as arguments, the first one is the lowest integer it might return, and the second integer is the highest. To produce a random number from 1 to 10, in Python, we would write code like this:

```
from random import *
my_dice_role ← randint(1, 10)
```

Python can also round decimal numbers by calling the round() function. It works the same way as the corresponding pseudocode function:

```
>>> round(8.6234, 1)
>>> 8.6
```

You may be surprised how often programmers require random numbers.

SUMMARY

Programs use variables and constants to hold values.
Variables and constants have identifiers (names) that are used to refer to them in the program.
Variables are able to have the value they contain changed during the execution of a program. The values within constants remain the same while the program is running.
In Python, variable names should be descriptive and consist of lower case words joined by underscores.
In Python, constant names should contain all capital letters. In Cambridge IGCSE and O Level Computer Science pseudocode, they should be preceded with the CONSTANT keyword.
It is important to know what data types your variables are using (Integer, Real, Char, String and Boolean). This can be checked by using the type() function in Python.
The input() function returns values from the user as String data types. If number inputs are required, the values returned must be cast into Integers or Floats using the int() or float() functions.
Mathematical operators can be used with values held in numeric variables.
Random numbers can be generated with randint() and decimals rounded with the round() function.

END-OF-CHAPTER TASKS

1 Program a system that outputs a random number from 1 to 6 inclusive.

You will need to import Python's random module in the first line of your program like this:

```
import random
```

To obtain a random number and store it in a variable called my_random_number, use this code:

```
my_random_number = random.randint(a,b)
```

where a is the first possible random number and b is the highest possible random number.

2 Complete the program below that inputs the time from a 24-hour clock in the format *hrs.mins* (e.g. 18.25) and outputs the time in 12-hour format (e.g. 6.25). You do not need to add 'am' or 'pm' to the output.

```
time24 = float(input('Provide the time in the form 18.25: '))
if time24 < 13.0:
    print(time24)   # The input is in the correct format
else:
    # Your code goes here
```

> **TIP**
>
> The function round(num, a) takes a float num and the number of decimal places to round it to.

3 a Write a program that inputs the side-length of a triangle (in pixels). As output, the turtle should draw an equilateral triangle on the screen with the required dimensions.

The input should be the length of the similar sides, s, and the similar angles, a. The length of the base, b, is not required.

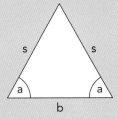

b Now try to produce a new version of your program that can draw isosceles triangles.

> Chapter 3
Algorithm design tools

IN THIS CHAPTER YOU WILL:

- learn the difference between the three programming constructs: sequence, selection and iteration
- learn how to use flowcharts and pseudocode when designing algorithms
- learn the main symbols used in flowcharts
- learn about the preferred format used in pseudocode.

Introduction

Many sporting activities make use of a limited range of approaches. Racket sports – such as badminton, for example – consist of a surprisingly limited number of different shots. Drop shots close to the net, long cleared shots to the back of the court and hard-driven shots account for a large proportion of the shots used in a game. The skill is in combining those three shots effectively to win the game.

Programming also makes use of a limited range of constructs to achieve complex tasks. Like a good badminton player, who combines different shots to win a game, an effective programmer will combine different constructs to produce efficient programs.

3.1 Programming constructs

Python and other procedural languages make use of three basic programming constructs: sequence, selection and iteration. Combining these constructs provides a programmer with the tools required to solve logical problems.

Sequence

In programming, sequence is the order in which the lines of code are written, usually top to bottom. The program will execute (run) the first line of code before moving to the second and subsequent lines. See Chapter 6 for more details.

Selection

Often your programs will perform different processes dependent on user input or the outcome from evaluating a condition. Consider a system designed to provide access to the school network based on when a user inputs a username and password. The system would need to follow a different path if the user inputs an incorrect password or username. See Chapter 7 for more details.

Iteration

It is common for a program to perform identical processes. Consider the turtle drawing a square in the last chapter. A line is drawn, followed by a right turn, four times. To repeat instructions, we can put them in a loop. Repeating instructions is referred to as iteration. Whenever you are copying and pasting lines of code, it is a strong indication that some sort of iteration is appropriate. See Chapter 8 for more details.

3.2 Design tools

When you design programs, it is normal to plan the logic of the program before you start to code the solution. The first step in the design process is to break down the problem into smaller problems. When we do this it is called decomposition.

KEY WORDS

construct: a method of controlling the order in which the statements in an algorithm are executed.

sequence: code is executed in the order it is written.

selection: code follows a different sequence based on what condition is chosen.

iteration: code repeats a certain sequence a number of times depending on certain conditions.

decomposition: a computational thinking skill that involves thinking about large tasks and breaking them down into smaller tasks.

TIP

Decomposition is one of the most important computational thinking skills to learn. This is when you break down a problem or system into smaller, more manageable parts. Use decomposition when you meet a new problem or feel overwhelmed by a complex problem.

KEY WORDS

algorithm: a process, instructions or set of rules to be followed during the execution of a program.

flowchart: a graphical representation of the sequence and logic of a program.

pseudocode: a way of unambiguously representing the sequence and logic of a program using both natural language and code-like statements.

The next stage is to design an **algorithm** for the individual problems. Two approaches that can be used to design algorithms are **flowcharts** and **pseudocode**.

To succeed in your course, you will be expected to have a working understanding of flowcharts and pseudocode. You will need to be able to use them to explain the logic of your solutions to given tasks. Both methods are used throughout this book.

3.3 Flowcharts

Flowcharts are graphical representations of the logic of the intended system. They make use of symbols to represent operations or processes and are joined by lines indicating the sequence of operations. Table 3.1 details the symbols used:

Symbol	Notes	Examples
Terminator	The START or STOP (or end) of a system.	START STOP
Input or output	Use when INPUT is required from the user or OUTPUT is being sent to the user.	INPUT number OUTPUT result
Process	A process within the system. Beware of making the process too generic. For example, a process entitled 'Calculate Average' would be too generic. It needs to indicate the values used to calculate the average.	result ← A * B average ← (A+B+C+D)/4

(continued)

Symbol	Notes	Examples
Logic flow	Joins two operations. The arrowhead indicates the flow of logic through the program. Iteration (looping) can be indicated by arrows returning to an earlier process in the flowchart.	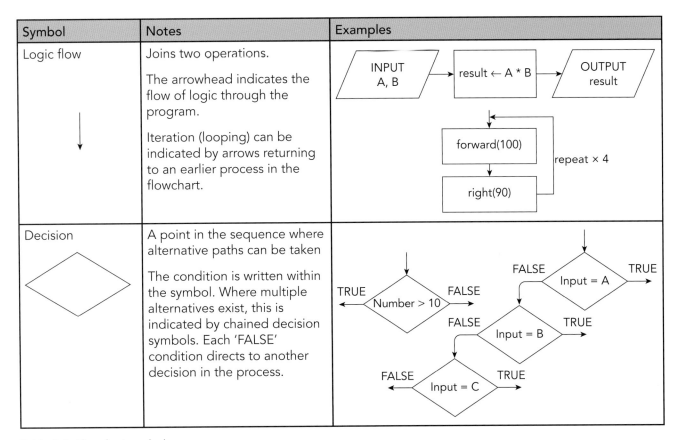
Decision	A point in the sequence where alternative paths can be taken The condition is written within the symbol. Where multiple alternatives exist, this is indicated by chained decision symbols. Each 'FALSE' condition directs to another decision in the process.	

Table 3.1: Flowchart symbols

PRACTICE TASK 3.1

Constructs

Which of the symbols in the first column of the Table 3.1 are used to represent the following constructs:

a   iteration   b   selection   c   sequence?

3.4 Pseudocode

Pseudocode is another way of describing the logic and sequence of an algorithm. It uses keywords and constructs, similar to those used in programming languages, but without the need for a strict use of **syntax**. Pseudocode allows the logic of the system to be defined in a programming language-independent format. This can then be coded using any programming language. Hence, the flow diagrams and pseudocode in this book are often almost entirely the same as those used in the Visual Basic and Java sister books of the series.

KEY WORD

syntax: the specific words, symbols and constructs defined for use by a particular language. It is the equivalent of grammar in creative writing.

Pseudocode follows a number of underlying principles:

- Use capital letters for keywords close to those used in programming languages.

- Use lower case letters for natural language descriptions.

- Use indentation to show the start and end of blocks of code statements, primarily when using selection and iteration.

One of the advantages of learning to program using Python is that the actual coding language is structured in a similar way to natural language and therefore closely resembles pseudocode. Python IDEs such as IDLE, Thonny and Wing IDE also automatically indent instructions where appropriate.

Pseudocode example

The following pseudocode is for an algorithm that accepts the input of two numbers. These values are added together and the result is stored in a memory area called answer. The value in answer is then displayed to the user.

```
INPUT number1
INPUT number2
answer ← number1 + number2
OUTPUT answer
```

Code snippet 3.1

Note the use of ← to show the passing of values. This is pseudocode's **assignment** operator. In pseudocode the equals symbol (=) is used to compare values. It is important to note that in Python, the equals symbol is used for assignment and two equals symbols (==) are used to compare values. The assignment operator attaches a value – in this case the sum of number1 and number2 – to a variable name, often referred to as an **identifier**.

> ## KEY WORDS
>
> **assignment:** passing a value, such as some text or a number, to a named variable.
>
> **identifier:** the unique name given to elements of a program, such as variables, constants and functions. An identifier can then be used to represent the named element elsewhere in the program.

PRACTICE TASKS 3.2–3.3

3.2 Identifiers

How many identifiers are there in the pseudocode in Code snippet 3.1?

3.3 A first flowchart

Construct a flowchart to represent the pseudocode example in Code snippet 3.1.

> ### TIP
>
> Do not forget that two terminators are required in flowcharts. These do not appear in pseudocode.

3.5 Effective use of flowcharts and pseudocode

Due to their universal nature, flowcharts and pseudocode are used extensively in the syllabuses.

The aim of this book is to help you to learn how to code effective systems in Python. The following chapters make use of flowcharts and pseudocode to define the logic of systems before moving on to specific Python solutions.

Learning how to explain the logic of programs by using these design techniques is important for your preparation in using the languages of the future. Programming language syntax is likely to change but the need for effective computational thinking will remain.

> **TIP**
>
> After completing a flowchart or pseudocode, it is a good idea to try and follow it through one step at a time in the same way a computer would. Working through your algorithm in this way will help you to identify if you have any missing steps.

PRACTICE TASK 3.4

Write pseudocode

Write a pseudocode version of the algorithm shown in Flowchart 3.1.

```
          START
            │
            ▼
    fullname ← ' '
            │
            ▼
        INPUT
      firstname
       lastname
            │
            ▼
fullname ← firstname + lastname
            │
            ▼
        OUTPUT
       fullname
            │
            ▼
          STOP
```

Flowchart 3.1

SUMMARY

Programmers make use of three constructs when writing code:

- sequence: the logical order in which code is executed

- selection: branching of code onto different paths based on certain conditions

- iteration: repetition of sections of code.

Before coding a program, it is crucial to design an appropriate algorithm.

If a program is to refer to a value, the value must be assigned to a variable with an identifier (a variable name).

Flowcharts are graphical representations of the logic of a system. They make use of symbols to represent operations or processes, and lines indicate the sequence of operations.

Pseudocode describes the logic of a system in a similar way to a programming language but without such strict syntax requirements.

END-OF-CHAPTER TASKS

This is a reference chapter. There are no end-of-chapter questions because we want to get you back to programming as soon as possible. In the following chapters, especially the chapters on Sequence (Chapter 6), Selection (Chapter 7) and Iteration (Chapter 8), you will get plenty of opportunities to try out what you have learnt in this chapter.

> # Chapter 4
> # Subroutines

IN THIS CHAPTER YOU WILL:

- learn how to use subroutines in programming
- learn how to pass values to subroutines and handle values passed back from subroutines
- learn how to design, program and use a procedure
- learn how to design, program and use a function
- learn about variable scope.

Introduction

Imagine you are writing a program that has 100 users who want to be able to change their name. Imagine that to do this you had to write your code like this:

```
If user1 wants to change their name:
    <code that asks for user1's new name and then edits it>
If user2 wants to change their name:
    <code that asks for user2's new name and then edits it>
If user3 wants to change their name:
    <code that asks for user3's new name and then edits it>
...
If user100 wants to change their name:
    <code that asks for user100's new name and then edits it>
```

Your program would be very long and the chances of making a mistake would be high. Finding errors would also be very tedious. Thankfully, we do not need to write code in this way. We can write one smaller program, within our larger program, that can be called whenever any user needs to have their name changed. These smaller programs are called subroutines.

Now imagine you have programmed a video game that releases a ball every time you press the space bar. This should happen in the same way every time the space bar is pressed. What you need is a small program that is called, inside your main game program, that can be somehow attached to keyboard presses. These small programs are, of course, called subroutines.

In this chapter, you will learn about two types of subroutines: functions and procedures. In Chapter 5, an optional chapter, you will learn how to write programs with GUIs and how to attach subroutines to keyboard presses.

4.1 Subroutines

A **subroutine** is code that performs a specific task that can be called from anywhere in the rest of your program. All subroutines in Python require an identifier (a name) and the keyword def, which is short for define. For example, in the code below (Code snippet 4.1), my_function is the identifier:

```
def my_function():
    # code that carries out the purpose of my_function
```

Code snippet 4.1

A subroutine can then be called in the rest of the program as often as is required by its identifier. After the subroutine has completed execution, the main program carries on as normal.

KEY WORD

subroutine: subroutines provide an independent section of code that can be called from another routine while the program is running. In this way, subroutines can be used to perform common tasks within a program.

Advantages of using subroutines

The ability to call subroutines from the main code offers a number of advantages:

- **The subroutine can be called when needed**. A single block of code can be used many times in our programs. Being able to reuse code avoids the need to repeat identical code sequences, which shortens our programs and makes them easier to read.

- **There is only one section of code to debug**. If an error is located in a subroutine, only the individual subroutine needs to be debugged. If the code had been repeated throughout the main program, every occurrence would need to be found and changed.

- **There is only one section of code to update**. If we improve or extend our subroutine, the benefits are available everywhere the subroutine is called in our program.

- **Button presses can be used to call various subroutines**. You will learn about this in the optional chapter, Chapter 5.

Types of subroutine

> **TIP**
>
> It is important to know that different programming languages define functions and procedures differently. This is why when you look up the definitions of these two words online you may find different definitions. The descriptions given in this chapter are those used in the syllabuses. In Python all subroutines are simply called functions.

Two main types of subroutine exist: **functions** and **procedures**.

- Functions contain a mini program that can be **called** by the main program. They may need to be **passed** some values. These are called **parameters**. They then return a computed value back to the main program. Here is a pseudocode example of a program that defines a function and then calls it:

```
FUNCTION add_two_numbers(a, b)
    sum ← a + b
    RETURN sum
ENDFUNCTION

my_number ← add_two_numbers(5,6)
```

Code snippet 4.2

add_two_numbers is the function identifier; a and b are the parameters and 5 and 6 are the **arguments** passed to the function. Alternatively, we could have output the return value, for example:

```
OUTPUT add_two_numbers(5,6)
```

KEY WORDS

function: a subroutine that can receive multiple parameters and returns a single value. A function always returns a value through its identifier.

procedure: a subroutine that can receive and return multiple parameters. It may or may not return a value. If values are returned, they are returned via parameters.

call: to activate a subroutine. To do this, you specify the subroutine's name and, optionally, parameters.

pass: a subroutine may require some values to compute with. When this is the case we say the values are passed to the subroutine.

parameters: data or values that are passed to, or received from, a subroutine.

arguments: when a program calls a subroutine, it may need to pass some values to it. Parameters are the names of the variables. Arguments are the actual values passed.

- Procedures are small sections of code that can be reused. They are just the same as functions but they do not return a value to the main program. In pseudocode, a procedure is named and takes the form:

```
PROCEDURE ... ENDPROCEDURE
```

They are called by using the CALL statement.

The CALL statement is used to execute the procedure. However, any values required by the procedure must be passed to it at the same time:

```
CALL my_procedure
```

Here is a pseudocode example of a procedure and a call to it:

```
PROCEDURE add_two_numbers(a, b)
    sum ← a + b
    OUTPUT sum
ENDPROCEDURE
CALL add_two_numbers(5,6)
```

Code snippet 4.3

PRACTICE TASK 4.1

Sum

In both the function (Code snippet 4.2) and the procedure (Code snippet 4.3), sum is calculated from the same two arguments.

a   What value is returned by the function add_two_numbers()?

b   What value is output by the procedure add_two_numbers()?

A complicated programming task can be made simpler if it is broken down into smaller problems. These smaller tasks can often be coded in a subroutine. A good sign that this is an appropriate thing to do is when you find yourself copying and pasting code. Breaking problems down into smaller problems is called decomposition. Going through a program and pulling out common sections of code into subroutines is called refactoring. If you decompose your problems and refactor your programs, you will benefit from all the advantages that subroutines can bring to your projects.

Another reason for putting sections of code into a subroutine is to hide complexity. This is abstraction. Imagine that a program required us to find the fourth highest scorer in a game. Instead of adding a lot of complicated code to the main part of the program we could, instead, call a subroutine with a meaningful name such as get_fourth_place_player(). A person reading the program can see what is being done and then look up how it is being performed if they wish to know. Abstraction is a computational thinking skill. You are using abstraction when you identify key elements in a problem and ignore unnecessary details.

Decomposition and abstraction often go hand in hand when writing programs. For example, an experienced programmer may spot a minor problem that they want to solve later and, instead of writing the code straight away, may write a function call to a function they will write later.

KEY WORDS

decomposition: a computational thinking skill that involves thinking about large tasks and breaking them down into smaller tasks.

refactoring: the process of pulling out repeating lines of code into subroutines and loops.

abstraction: a computational thinking skill that involves spotting key information in a problem and hiding unnecessary information. This is most often done by programmers when details of an algorithm are abstracted into a subroutine.

TIP

Try not to be confused between 'parameter' and 'argument'. They are often used interchangeably. Strictly speaking, parameters are used in the function definition. When we call a function, we pass it arguments.

4.2 Programming a function

The syntax for defining a function in Python and then calling it is shown here:

```
def square(side_length):
    # code to draw a square goes here

square(50)
```

Code snippet 4.4

PRACTICE TASK 4.2

Square function

Write a turtle program that uses a function called 'square' to draw a square with sides of length 100.

DEMO TASK 4.1

Circumference

a   *Write a function that will be passed the radius of a circle and output the circumference of the circle with this radius.*

b   *Write a program that includes the function from **a** and then outputs the circumference of a circle with radius 10.*

Solution

For part **a**, we can write the pseudocode fairly quickly. The function needs:

1   a meaningful name that tells us what it does (for example, calculate_circumference) and

2   to be passed the radius.

The code within the function needs to calculate the circumference of a circle and return that value like this:

```
FUNCTION calculate_circumference(radius)
    RETURN 2 * 3.142 * radius
ENDFUNCTION
```

Code snippet 4.5

The pseudocode for part **b** is one additional line. Here is the whole program:

```
FUNCTION calculate_circumference(radius)
    RETURN 2 * 3.142 * radius
ENDFUNCTION

OUTPUT calculate_circumference(10)
```

Code snippet 4.6

TIP

Notice how, when calling a 'procedure' in Python, there is no need to use a CALL keyword, as is required in the pseudocode used in the syllabuses. This is because, in Python, all subroutines are treated as functions, and the function name (with arguments, if required) is enough to call it.

CONTINUED

We can now use the pseudocode to write our Python program:

```
def calculate_circumference(radius):
    return 2 * 3.142 * radius

print(calculate_circumference(10))
```

Code snippet 4.7

PRACTICE TASKS 4.3–4.5

Write pseudocode solutions for the following tasks. Then write and test a Python implementation of each solution.

4.3 Number squared

Write a function that takes as a parameter a single integer value and returns the square of that number. For example, if passed the value 4, your function should return 16. The function should be called from your main program subroutine and output the answer.

4.4 Highest number

Write a function that takes two numbers as parameters and returns the highest number. The function should be called from your main program and output the answer.

The code you will need to do the comparison in the function is:

```
if number1 > number2:
    return number1
else:
    return number2
```

4.5 Password number

Write a function that can check if a password number is between 1000 and 9999 inclusive. It will take the password number as a parameter value and return the word 'PASS' or the word 'FAIL' depending on whether the password falls within the required range.

Your function should be called from the main program and output the answer.

TIP

For Practice Task 4.5, use the same if ... else structure as in Practice Task 4.4. You will learn more about selection in Chapter 7.

CHALLENGE TASK 4.1

Draw a flower

Design a turtle program that draws a flower by using the turtle circle function. To get access to this turtle function, you do not need to write it. You just need to import the turtle library in the normal way. Your program should pass to the circle function the radius, a value of 50, and then draw five circles, turning 72° after drawing each one.

Returning two values from a function

It is easy to return two values in pseudocode:

```
RETURN value1, value2
```

In Python, this is accomplished in the same way. Look at this interactive session to see how this works:

INTERACTIVE SESSION

```
>>> def my_function():
        return 1,2
>>> a,b = my_function()
>>> print(a)
1
>>> print(b)
2
>>>
```

PRACTICE TASK 4.6

Circle properties

Write a function that takes as a parameter the radius of a circle. Your function should return both the circumference and the area of the circle. Your main program should call this function and pass it the value 50. It should then print out both the circumference and the radius.

CHALLENGE TASK 4.2

Circle properties

Amend your program from Practice Task 4.6 so that the main part of the program asks the user to input the radius of a circle. Your new program should then pass this value to your function before outputting the circumference and the area of the circle.

SKILLS FOCUS 4.1

VARIABLE SCOPE

The point at which you declare or initialise a variable in your program will determine which parts of the program are able to use that variable.

Global variables can be accessed from any part of the program. They are used for variables that need to be accessed from anywhere in your program. To be a global variable, it must be declared outside of all subroutines. It is good practice to declare all your global variables at the start of your code.

KEY WORD

global variable: a variable that can be accessed from any routine within the program.

CONTINUED

The values held in global variables can be accessed by all functions. However, if the function is going to change the value stored in the global variable, that value must be re-declared using the `global` keyword (see Code snippet 4.8).

Local variables can only be accessed in the code element in which they are declared. A variable declared inside a function can only be accessed by the code in that particular function. Using local variables reduces the possibility of accidentally changing variable values in other parts of your program.

In the following Python example, there is one global variable and one local variable.

```
player_score = 0

def update_player_score():
    global player_score
result = 5
    if player_score < result:
        player_score = player_score+1
```

Code snippet 4.8

Questions

1 What are the names of the global and local variables?
2 Why is the `global` keyword required inside the `update_player_score()` function?
3 When using a global variable inside a function, in what situation would the `global` keyword not be required?

Note how `player_score` is re-declared at the start of the function with the `global` keyword. This is because the value of this global variable might be changed by the `update_player_score()` function.

PRACTICE TASK 4.7

Global name

Write a Python program that stores a user's name in a global variable called `name` and a function that allows the user to edit it. Your first line of code should be:

```
name = 'Jon Jones'
```

After calling your function, your program should print out the corrected name.

4.3 Programming a procedure

The Python code for a procedure is similar to that used for a function. Remember, however, that procedures, just like functions, can contain parameters. The key difference in the syllabus definitions is that procedures do not return a value, whereas functions always do. In the interactive session below, empty brackets are used to show that no parameters are required by the subroutine.

INTERACTIVE SESSION

```
>>> def greeting():
        print('Hello', 'Hello', 'Hello')
>>> greeting()
Hello Hello Hello
>>>
```

Notice how the `greeting()` function contains the built-in function, `print()`.

PRACTICE TASK 4.8

Draw a star

a Write a pseudocode algorithm for a procedure called `star()` that instructs a turtle robot to draw a star by moving forwards 50 and turning right 144° five times.

b Test that your algorithm works by programming the procedure in Python and providing a call to the procedure.

SUMMARY

Subroutines provide an independent section of code that can be called from anywhere in the rest of your program while the program is running. In this way, subroutines can be used to perform common tasks within a program. A subroutine can be called multiple times throughout the program.
Because a subroutine is separate from the main program, it is easier to debug, maintain or update than repetitive code within the main program.
Subroutines can be passed values known as parameters.
A procedure is used to separate out repetitive code from the main program.
A function is a type of subroutine that returns values to the main program.
Variables that can be accessed from any routine within the program are called global variables.
Variables that can only be accessed in the code element in which they are declared are called local variables.

END-OF-CHAPTER TASKS

Select either a function or procedure to complete the following tasks. Design your solution using pseudocode before coding and testing your design in Python.

1 Write a subroutine that will convert a time measured in seconds and return the same time in minutes and seconds. Then complete your program by adding the code that will call the subroutine, pass it a single integer value that represents the number of seconds, and print this out.

For example, if the subroutine is passed 190 seconds, it would return 3 minutes 10 seconds.

2 Write a subroutine that will convert measurements of speed from kilometres per hour (kph) to miles per hour (mph). Your main program will need to pass the subroutine the speed value in kilometres per hour and the subroutine will return the same speed in mile per hour. Finally print out the speed in mph. (1.60934 kilometres per hour = 1 mile per hour)

3 Write a turtle program that contains a procedure which draws a square with side length 100. Your program should repeatedly draw a square and turn right 60°. In total your program should draw six squares.

4 Write a program that will calculate and output the amount of paint that is required to paint a wall. The main program will make use of a subroutine to complete the task.

The subroutine will be called by the main program and passed the height and width of the wall.

The subroutine will be required to calculate:

1 The exact amount of paint required. 1 litre of paint can cover 8 square metres of wall.

2 The number of tins of paint needed to paint the wall. Paint can only be obtained in 5 litre tins.

The subroutine will return two values:

1 The exact amount of paint required in litres.

2 The number of tins required to paint the wall.

TIP

For Task 4, the `ceil()` function can round up numbers to the nearest whole number and the `floor()` function can round down numbers but you will need to import the `math` library to use these functions.

`round()` is available without importing `math` and does what you would expect.

> # Chapter 5
GUI
applications

IN THIS CHAPTER YOU WILL:

- learn how to produce and save GUI applications

- learn how to write windowed applications using the built-in tkinter GUI module

- learn how to add widgets to a GUI application

- learn how to lay out widgets in an application window

- learn how to call a function with a button press.

Note: GUI applications are not covered in the syllabuses, therefore, the whole of this chapter is optional. Any Further Information boxes in this chapter refer to material that is not necessary to understand in this optional chapter.

Introduction

In Chapter 1, you were introduced to interactive mode and script-based programming. This optional chapter shows you how to create programs that appear in windows and have features such as buttons and text boxes. The syllabuses do not require that you produce applications with GUIs. However, you may want to produce more visually interesting and professional looking solutions to problems. Doing so will also make you a more flexible programmer as you reformat your scripts into GUI applications.

In future chapters, normal script-based solutions are going to be referred to as *text-based solutions* and programs that appear in windows are going to be called *GUI solutions*. After this chapter, you will often be asked to produce two solutions, first a text-based one and then a GUI solution. Producing the GUI programs are optional extensions that go beyond the scope of the syllabuses.

5.1 Make your first application in a window with a button

By importing the tkinter module, it is easy to produce visually rich GUIs that use buttons to interact with the program.

Tkinter is an example of a GUI toolkit and is provided as part of the standard library when you install Python. This means you already have access to the objects and methods required to make GUI applications. To add these elements to your programs, you just need to do these extra tasks:

1   Import the tkinter module.
2   Create the main tkinter window.
3   Add one or more tkinter **widgets** to your application.
4   Enter the **main event loop**, which listens to and acts upon events triggered by the user.

By following these four steps, you are turning your program into an **event-driven system**. This means that the whole application runs in an **infinite loop**. This is the main event loop referred to in step 4 above and started by the last line of code below. Once the main event loop is started, the application opens in its own window. This application now constantly 'listens' for user interaction, such as pressing buttons or choosing an item in a drop-down menu.

To create the application shown in Figure 5.1, copy the code below (Code snippet 5.1) into a new script and save it as `hello-gui.py` into your Python code folder.

Note: A button can call a function by name after `command=` in the button definition code.

KEY WORDS

tkinter: a module that is provided as part of the standard library in Python. It provides tools to help the programmer build applications that have buttons, textboxes, etc.

widget: interface items such as buttons and text boxes that can be used to build GUIs.

main event loop: a loop that iterates the whole time the program is running. Its main job is to 'listen' for user input and to call subroutines to handle the input.

event-driven system: an application that runs in an infinite loop and can react to events that occur while the program is running, such as user input or a sprite colliding with the wall of a window.

infinite loop: a type of iteration that has no termination condition and so goes on forever. This is sometimes created accidently by an error in a loop condition. There are also genuine uses, such as when an app has to always be listening for button presses.

```
# hello-gui.py

# Import everything required from the tkinter module
from tkinter import *

# Function called by clicking my_button:
def change_text():
    my_label.config(text='Hello World')

# Create the main tkinter window
window = Tk()
window.title('My Application')

# Add an empty tkinter label widget and place it in a grid layout
my_label = Label(window, width=25, height=1, text='')
my_label.grid(row=0, column=0)

# Add a tkinter button widget, place it in the grid layout
# and attach the change_text() function
my_button = Button(window, text='Say Hi', width=10, command=change_text)
my_button.grid(row=1, column=0)

# Enter the main event loop
window.mainloop()
```

Code snippet 5.1

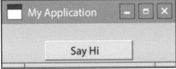

Figure 5.1: A GUI application with a button

After running the code, press the 'Say Hi' button to see how this small application works. Notice how the button is linked to the change_text() function by command= in the button definition.

> **Further Information:**
>
> The tkinter module provides classes, objects and methods that you can access and use in your own applications. Tkinter is written using object-oriented programming (OOP), which is beyond the scope of the syllabuses. In OOP programs, object methods are called using the dot operator. This can be seen in Code snippet 5.1 in the change_text() function where the config() method is applied to the label widget. Here it is again:
>
> ```
> my_label.config(text='Hello World')
> ```
>
> If you want to learn more about OOP you might like to work through *Python: Building Big Apps*, a level 3 book in the Coding Club series, or perhaps try *Introduction to Programming with Greenfoot* by Michael Kölling, which teaches Java programming in a very interactive, game-based way.

When designing the layout of widgets in GUI applications, you can use the `grid()` method (see Table 5.1). This organises as many cells as you require in your window using a coordinate system. Note how the numbers start from zero in the top left corner of the window:

row=0, column=0	row=0, column=1	row=0, column=2
row=1, column=0	row=1, column=1	row=1, column=2
row=2, column=0	row=2, column=1	row=2, column=2

Table 5.1: Layout using grid() method

It is possible to further arrange tkinter widgets by grouping them in frames.

5.2 Other tkinter widgets you can use in your applications

In this section you will find a few other useful widget examples you might want to include in your applications. These code snippets should all be added after `window = Tk()` and above `window.mainloop()` as indicated by the comment in the following recipe for an empty tkinter window (a recipe is another name for a piece of code that you use frequently):

A recipe for an empty tkinter window

```
from tkinter import *

window = Tk()
window.title('My Application')

# widget code goes here

window.mainloop()
```

Code snippet 5.2

A text entry box with a label

```
Label(window, text='Name:').grid(row=0, column=0)
my_text_box = Entry(window, width=15)
my_text_box.grid(row=0, column=1)
```

Code snippet 5.3

Two frames

```
frame1 = Frame(window,height=20,width=100,bg='green')
frame1.grid(row=0, column=0)
frame2 = Frame(window,height=20,width=100,bg='red')
frame2.grid(row=1, column=1)
```

Code snippet 5.4

A drop-down menu

```
options = (1,2,3)
my_variable_object = IntVar() # access the value with .get()
my_variable_object.set('choose:')
my_dropdown = OptionMenu(window, my_variable_object, *options)
my_dropdown.grid()
```

Code snippet 5.5

PRACTICE TASK 5.1

Tkinter widgets

Open a new script and add the code from the empty window recipe (Code snippet 5.2). Save this script and then add the code for each example widget, one at a time, to see how they appear.

Do not worry about the widgets in your application doing anything at this stage. Just focus on the design and layout.

DEMO TASK 5.1

Pet gender GUI application

Create a radio button application that gives the user a choice of two radio buttons to indicate the gender of their pet. Your application should align the tkinter widgets to the left (West) side of a `grid()` *cell. It should also access the value selected in the radio buttons using a tkinter* `StringVar()` *object and display the choice made (Figure 5.2).*

Figure 5.2: A GUI application with two radio buttons

Solution

Here is the Python code that demonstrates how to produce a GUI for this very simple, one function, program.

```
# gender-gui.py
from tkinter import *

# Functions go here:
def change_text():
    my_label.config(text=gender.get())

# GUI code goes here:
# Create the main tkinter window
window = Tk()
window.title('My Application')
```

CONTINUED

```
# Add an empty tkinter label widget and place it in a grid layout
my_label = Label(window, width=25, height=1, text='')
my_label.grid(row=0, column=0)

# Add a tkinter button widget, place it in the grid layout
# and attach the change_text() function
my_button = Button(window, text='Submit', width=10, command=change_text)
my_button.grid(row=1, column=0)

# Create a tkinter string variable object for the radio buttons
gender = StringVar()
# Add two radio button widgets
# Use optional sticky argument to align left
radio1 = Radiobutton(window, text='Female', variable=gender, value='female')
radio1.grid(row=2, column=0, sticky=W)
radio1.select() # pre-selects this radio button for the user
radio2 = Radiobutton(window, text='Male', variable=gender, value='male')
radio2.grid(row=3, column=0, sticky=W)


# Enter the main loop event
window.mainloop()
```

Code snippet 5.6

PRACTICE TASKS 5.2–5.3

5.2 Compass points

a   Study the code that inserts the radio buttons in Code snippet 5.6. Which bit of code places them on the left side of the app?

b   How would you move them to the right side of the app?

c   Amend gender-gui.py by aligning the radio buttons to the East and see what happens when you run it again.

5.3 Drop-down menu

Rewrite the radio button application in Demo Task 5.1, but replace the radio buttons with a simple drop-down menu.

5.3 Choosing a text-based or GUI application

From Chapter 6 onwards, answers to problems are given as either text-based applications or GUI applications and often both.

Text-based programs more accurately reflect the programming style of the syllabuses. Text-based applications do not involve the additional complexity of having to reference tkinter's GUI widgets.

However, GUI applications will offer a richer visual experience and produce systems similar to those that are commercially available.

It is suggested that you make use of both types of applications. This will best support the development of your computational thinking. A text-based answer is always provided to problems presented in this book in the solutions.

CHALLENGE TASK 5.1

Two-way converter

Design the algorithms for and build a GUI application that takes a speed in either mph or kph and converts to the other one.

Your application should look like Figure 5.3:

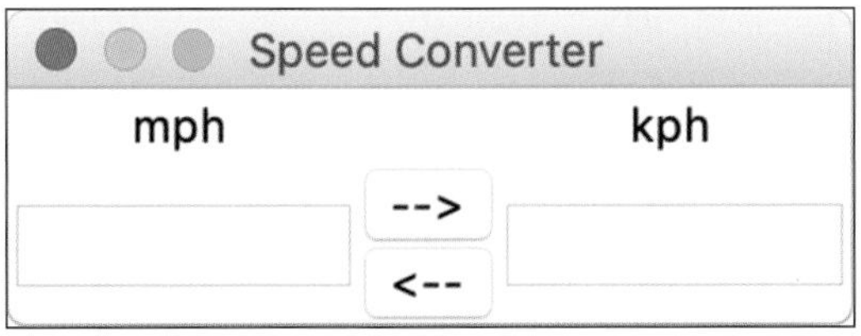

Figure 5.3: A GUI application speed converter

Your application should function like this:

The user can enter a number in either text entry box, and then press the appropriate arrow button to display the converted speed in the other text entry box.

SUMMARY

There are three main styles of programming in Python 3:

- Interactive mode: quick tests and trials that can be programmed in the Python shell.

- Text-based: in script mode, text-based scripts can be saved so that your applications can be reused.

- GUI applications: by importing the tkinter library, visually rich applications can be produced in script mode.

GUI programs open in their own window and contain familiar widgets such as buttons and text boxes.

The tkinter module is a GUI library that is available in the standard Python 3 install.

Tkinter's grid method allows programmers to position widgets by using cell coordinates starting with (0,0) from the top left corner of a window or frame.

Text-based programs are all that is required by the syllabuses and closely match the logic of the algorithms they implement.

GUI programs provide a richer experience for the user but introduce added complexity for the programmer.

END-OF-CHAPTER TASKS

1 Amend the program from `hello-gui.py` (Code snippet 5.1) so that it has two buttons next to each other. Label the first one 'Say Hi' and label the second button 'Say Bye'. Try setting the width of the label and both the buttons to 10. Attach an appropriate function to your new button.

2 Amend your program from End-of-Chapter Task 1 so that the two buttons are stacked vertically.

3 Make a tiny keyboard that has a grid of 9 number buttons (1 to 9) and displays the result of pressing each number in a tkinter label widget:

4 Make a GUI with as many of the widgets as you can from Appendix 2. Do not worry about the widgets doing anything. Then experiment with laying them out in different ways.

> **TIP**
>
> For Task 3, it is best to put the number buttons in a frame. See Appendix 2 for how to do this.

> **TIP**
>
> You might like to store one of your answers to End-of-Chapter Task 4 as a template. When producing GUI applications in the future, you will be able to save yourself some typing by copying the code you need from your 'template' program.

> Chapter 6

Sequence and strings

Introduction

The order that things are done is very important in many situations. Imagine the mess if you cooked a meal in this order:

- Pour in the food.
- Heat the pot.
- Get the pot off the shelf.

It is the same in programming. If your program is to produce the correct results, it is also very important that the instructions are in the correct order. For example, to calculate the time it would take to complete a journey, we need to know the distance to be travelled and the intended speed. The first step would be to calculate the distance to be travelled. Without this data, the rest of the task could not be completed.

The sequence in which instructions are programmed can be crucial. Consider the following algorithm that is intended to do just this task:

Time = Distance / Speed

Speed = 12 kilometres per hour

Distance = 15 miles

A human would spot that the distance is in miles and the speed in kilometres per hour and convert one of them so that the units would match. A computer would not do this unless there were precise instructions. In fact, with the algorithm above, the computer would attempt to calculate the time in the first line and discover it does not have a speed or distance (it will not move to the second line until it has finished the first) and so, would stop running.

PRACTICE TASK 6.1

Correct the algorithm

Correct the algorithm given in the introduction so that a computer could follow the sequence of instructions and output the time the journey would take in hours.

6.1 Flowcharts and sequence

Flowcharts make designing **sequence** in **algorithms** obvious. The order in which things happen flows from the Start terminator symbol to the End terminator symbol. The flow of logic follows the arrows from Start to End.

KEY WORDS

flowchart: a graphical representation of the sequence and logic of a program.

sequence: code is executed in the order it is written.

algorithm: a process, instructions or set of rules to be followed during the execution of a program.

DEMO TASK 6.1

Arrival time flowchart

Design an algorithm that will calculate an estimated arrival time for an aeroplane journey. The steps in the process are:

Step 1 Obtain the distance between the two airports.

Step 2 Calculate the time it will take to complete the journey.

Step 3 Output the estimated journey time.

Solution

Flowchart 6.1 shows the flowchart that represents the above steps:

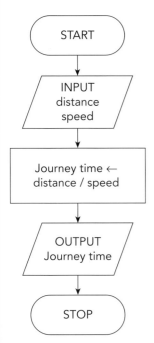

Flowchart 6.1

This task follows a simple linear process, so the flowchart that represents it will also follow a single path. Note the parallelogram symbols used to indicate the inputs and outputs. When you come to write the code for your programs, these symbols will help you identify when you need to obtain user input.

Step 2 'Calculate the time to complete the journey' left room for interpretation. It did not define what speed should be used to calculate the journey time. Different aircraft fly at different speeds, so it is likely that the user would be expected to input the speed to be used, but this step was not shown. Therefore our flowchart had to add this information because effective flowcharts leave no room for ambiguity.

TIP

While you are in the early stages of learning how to draw flowcharts, it is a good idea to keep checking back to Chapter 3 to make sure you get the symbols correct.

PRACTICE TASK 6.2

Journey time

Can you identify any other ambiguities in the flowchart in Flowchart 6.1?

CHALLENGE TASK 6.1

Journey time program

a   Write a Python implementation of the algorithm in Demo Task 6.1.

b   Have you found any more ambiguities while writing a working program?

6.2 Pseudocode and sequence

In this section, we will produce representations of algorithms using **pseudocode**. Pseudocode was introduced in Chapter 3. Here are the main ideas again:

- Use capital letters for keywords that are close to those used in programming languages.

- Use lower case letters for natural language descriptions.

- Use indentation to show the start and end of blocks of code.

The third bullet point does not apply in this chapter. This will be more important in the following chapters on selection and iteration.

KEY WORD

pseudocode: a way of unambiguously representing the sequence and logic of a program using both natural language and code-like statements.

Pseudocode example

The pseudocode below (Code snippet 6.1) is for an algorithm that accepts the input of two numbers. These values are added together and the result is stored in the variable called Answer. The value in Answer is then displayed to the user.

```
INPUT Number1
INPUT Number 2
Answer ← Number1 + Number2
OUTPUT Answer
```

Code snippet 6.1

Note the use of ← to show the passing of values to the variable identifier.

DEMO TASK 6.2

Arrival time in pseudocode

Write a pseudocode version of the flowchart algorithm produced in Demo Task 6.1. Here it is again:

> *Step 1 Obtain the distance between the two airports.*
>
> *Step 2 Calculate the time it will take to complete the journey.*
>
> *Step 3 Output the estimated journey time.*

Solution

Our first attempt may involve pulling the text from these steps and translating it into pseudocode. Just like when we drew the flowchart, we will soon notice that to calculate the journey time, we also need to input the speed:

```
INPUT distance
INPUT speed
journey_time ← distance / speed
OUTPUT journey_time
```

Code snippet 6.2

If we want to check our algorithm, we could write a text-based Python implementation, which would look like this:

```
distance = int(input('Distance between airports in kilometres: '))
speed = int(input('How fast is the plane in kilometres per hour: '))
journey_time = distance / speed
print(journey_time)
```

Code snippet 6.3

This is all very similar to the pseudocode except that we must remember that all user input in Python is provided as a string. Therefore, if we wish to use the numbers in calculations later in our program, we need to cast numbers that are input as text to either an integer or a float. For example:

```
users_int = int(input('Enter an integer: '))
users_float = float(input('Enter a decimal number: '))
```

Code snippet 6.4

TIP

When writing your own pseudocode, you can name variables as you wish, if they have not been given to you. It is quite normal to use the syntax that is used in your preferred programming language. However, note that the pseudocode in examination questions will not use underscore-separated lower case words like we do in Python.

It is important to remember that you must use the exact form of any variable names that are given in an examination question.

PRACTICE TASK 6.3

Triangle size

a   Write a pseudocode algorithm that asks a user for the side length of an
     equilateral triangle and then gets a turtle robot to draw it. (Each different
     instruction sent to the robot will be a separate output in pseudocode.)

b   Write a Python implementation of your algorithm.

6.3 Use of flowcharts and pseudocode in programming

Because of the universal nature of flowcharts and pseudocode, they are used
extensively in the syllabuses.

Learning how to show the logic of programs through the use of these design
techniques will be a crucial step in your examination preparation. More importantly,
it will also help with your preparation for using programming languages of the future.
Language syntax is likely to change in the future, but the need for effective logical and
computational thinking will remain.

6.4 String manipulation in Python

When drawing flowcharts and pseudocode, we do not have to worry too much about
how to join or change bits of text. When writing our code, we have to think about the
details such as the space between strings, line returns, and so on.

There are two places we are likely to want to format and manipulate text: when you
want to get user input and when we want to produce output. In Python, we use the
`input()` and `print()` functions for these two operations.

KEY WORD

string: a data
type that is used
to hold a portion
of text. As well as
letters, a string
can also include
numbers, spaces and
punctuation.

The input() function

The `input()` function can get input, which we know is always returned as a string.
However, it can also send a message to the console.

Examples:

```
input() # no message is given but the program waits for input
input('Enter an integer: ') # waits for input after a message
user_int = input('Enter an integer: ') # passes user input to a variable.
```

Code snippet 6.5

The print() function

The `print()` function is similar to the `input()` function, except that it does not
wait for input. Instead, it sends data to the console. To find out some of the things
that `print()` can do, open up your IDE and start an interactive session.

INTERACTIVE SESSION

First create two strings a and b:

```
>>> a = 'Happy'
>>> b = 'Birthday'
```

Then try out some of these code snippets. It is a good idea to try and guess what you think might happen in each case.

```
>>> print(a + b)
>>> print(a + ' ' + b + '!')
>>> print(a, b)
>>> print(a, b, '!')
>>> print(a*2, b)
>>> print(a*200)
>>> print(5*20)
>>> print('5 x 20 =',5*20)
>>> print(a,'\n',b)
>>> print(a, '\n', a,'\n', b)
>>> print('He said: "Happy Birthday!"')
>>> print("He said: 'Happy Birthday!'")
```

TIP

If you are using IDLE's Python shell, there is a quick and convenient way of copying previously typed code: try placing your cursor in the code you want to copy and then press the Return key. The code will be copied and pasted directly to the next code entry prompt. The copied code can then be amended before pressing Return to execute it.

PRACTICE TASK 6.4

Two answers

Give two different lines of Python code that will output each of the following strings:

a   Hello Hello Hello

b   Please enter your "firstname":

c   20 / 5 = 4

CHALLENGE TASK 6.2

Input problems

You are trying to fix a program that has just input two numbers: a = 5 and b = 7. In the next line, you want to ask the user to input whether the sum of their two numbers is correct. Here is the code so far:

```
a = input('Enter your first number: ')
b = input('Enter your second number: ')
confirm = input('Is the sum of your two numbers ' + a+b + '?')
```

Your program should give the correct answer, 12, and ask if it is correct. Explain what has gone wrong and suggest how to fix it.

Other string manipulation functions

In Table 6.1, you will find a summary of the main string manipulation methods you need to know and how to represent them in pseudocode. Unfortunately, the syllabus pseudocode system and Python code differ a little in all of these operations so you will have to be careful.

Operation	Pseudocode	Python	Return value
Length of a string	`LENGTH('Hello')`	`len('Hello')`	5
Upper case	`UPPER('Hello')`	`'Hello'.upper()`	HELLO
Lower case	`LOWER('Hello')`	`'Hello'.lower()`	hello
Get a substring	`SUBSTRING('Hello', 1, 3)`	`'Hello'[1:4]`	ell

Table 6.1: Basic string manipulation syntax

Length of strings

Both pseudocode and Python use a function that returns the number of characters in a string. The difference is purely in the name of the function.

Upper case

Pseudocode uses the `UPPER()` function in the way you would expect. Python on the other hand uses a method and so the syntax is different. Methods are attached to the code they are operating on with the dot operator, as shown in Table 6.1. The output though is the same as for pseudocode. (Methods come from classes, which is beyond the syllabuses.)

Lower case

Pseudocode uses the `LOWER()` function in the way you would expect. Python on the other hand uses a method and so the syntax is different. Methods are attached to the code they are operating on with the dot operator, as shown in Table 6.1. The output though is the same as for pseudocode. (Methods come from classes, which is beyond the syllabuses.)

Get a substring

Pseudocode is using a function called `SUBSTRING()`, which takes three parameters shown in the brackets in Figure 6.1:

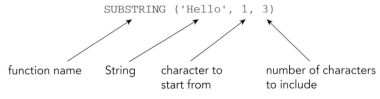

Figure 6.1: Explanation of pseudocode

To achieve the same output, Python does not have a **substring** function but instead uses a process called **'slicing'**. As well as having different syntax, the two parameters in the square brackets work in a different way (Figure 6.2):

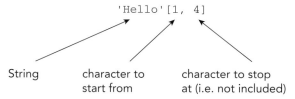

'Hello'[1, 4]

String   character to start from   character to stop at (i.e. not included)

Figure 6.2: Python syntax for slicing

KEY WORDS

substring: a portion of a string.

slicing: a facility in Python that allows a programmer to select a specified portion of a string.

On the plus side, in both pseudocode and Python, the first character is 0. (This is not the case for all languages; some number their strings from character 1.)

Further Information:

Slicing in Python is very flexible. Here are some other examples that show how to slice strings:

From character 2, to 2 characters from the end of a string:

```
>>> print('Hello'[1:-2])
el
```

From character 2, to the end of a string:

```
>>> print('Hello'[1:])
ello
```

The first three characters of a string:

```
>>> print('Hello'[:3])
Hel
```

PRACTICE TASK 6.5

String manipulation

In each of the following problems, `my_string` contains the string `"Hello Everyone"`.

a   Write the pseudocode and Python code that manipulates `my_string` to output: `"hello everyone"`.

b   Write the pseudocode and Python code that manipulates `my_string` to output: `"HELLO EVERYONE"`.

c   Write the pseudocode and Python code that manipulates `my_string` to output: `"lo Everyone"`.

d   Write the pseudocode and Python code that manipulates `my_string` to output: `"HELLO"`.

e   Write the pseudocode and Python code that counts the characters in `my_string`.

SUMMARY

Sequence is the logical order in which code is executed.
Before coding a program, it is crucial to design an appropriate algorithm using either a flowchart or pseudocode.
Flowcharts use a series of symbols to provide a visual representation of the logic of a program. The flow of the execution of the program is represented by flow lines with arrow heads.
Pseudocode is a method of describing the logic of a program by using written language.
Substrings can be obtained from strings using SUBSTRING() in pseudocode or slicing in Python.
There are methods and functions for finding the length of a string and converting a string to all lower case or all upper case.

END-OF-CHAPTER TASKS

1 Explain what the following flowchart symbols are used for:

  a   **b**   **c**

2 Casting is when we change a variable's data type from one form to another. If we want to input a number, we have to get the input from the keyboard as a string and then cast it with the int() or float() functions like this:

```
users_int = int(input('Enter an integer: '))
users_float = float(input('Enter a decimal number: '))
```

Rewrite the line of code below so that it saves the product of 5 and 2 as a string rather than as an integer:

```
my_integer = 5*2
```

3 a Design an algorithm using either pseudocode or a flowchart for a program that inputs a user's name and their five best 100m times in seconds. The program should then output their average and their PB (personal best) with the following text.

Example input:

```
Wayan
14.7
15.3
15.1
14.9
14.7
```

CONTINUED

Example output:

```
Hi Wayan, Here are your 100m statistics:
Your average 100m time is 14.94s
Your PB is 14.7s
```

b Write a Python implementation of your algorithm and test if it works.

TIP

For Task 3b, use the min() function which takes, as arguments, any amount of comma-separated numbers.

› Chapter 7
Selection

Introduction

We make decisions every day of our lives. If it is raining, I carry an umbrella. If I am thirsty, I drink some water. If I am stuck indoors and I want some fun, I write a computer program!

Systems often need to be programmed to make decisions depending on the input received. For example, an automatic door will open if it detects that someone wishes to enter and will shut when no one is detected. Programs like these appear to be able to make decisions based on input, but the reality is that the system has been designed using logical **selection** techniques. In Python, and many other languages, we achieve this by the use of programming techniques known as IF statements.

7.1 IF statements

If the process for an automatic door was written down, it might appear as: 'If a person is detected then open the door, otherwise close it.' This is very similar to coding an **IF statement**.

In a flowchart, the symbol used to indicate a decision is a diamond. The diamond contains information about the criteria and normally has two exit routes indicating the True and False paths (this is known as a **Boolean** condition).

Flowchart 7.1 includes the decision symbol and the True and False paths have been indicated. When this flowchart is programmed, this decision symbol will become an IF statement. Once the appropriate action has been performed, the logic flow returns back to 'Check for person at door' and the input is again evaluated by the IF statement.

> ## KEY WORDS
>
> **selection:** code follows a different sequence based on what condition is chosen.
>
> **IF statements:** a statement that allows a program to follow or ignore a sequence of code depending on a Boolean condition.
>
> **Boolean:** describes an operator, function or variable that only deals with True or False.

Flowchart 7.1

Below (Code snippet 7.1) is the pseudocode IF statement for Flowchart 7.1 (notice how closely the pseudocode matches our initial description in plain English):

```
IF person ← True
  THEN
    Open Door
  ELSE
    Close Door
ENDIF
```

Code snippet 7.1

Not all IF statements have an alternative action. Therefore, the ELSE may not always be needed. For example, a program used to calculate the cost of a train journey could apply a discount if the passenger is a child. The pseudocode would look like this:

```
discount ← 0.5
INPUT ticket_price


IF ticket for child
  THEN
    ticket_price ← ticket_price * discount
ENDIF


OUTPUT ticket_price
```

Code snippet 7.2

PRACTICE TASK 7.1

Ticket discounts

Write a Python script that implements the pseudocode ticket discount algorithm (Code snippet 7.2).

CHALLENGE TASK 7.1

Ticket discount flowchart

Draw a flowchart version of the ticket discount algorithm (Code snippet 7.2). You will need to decide what to do with the decision diamond when the algorithm has only an IF and no Else.

7.2 Logical operators

In the automatic door example, the only possible inputs were 'detected' or 'not detected'. An air-conditioning system, however, will receive continuous temperature data and perform actions based on a variety of temperature data. A program that calculates exam grades will need to calculate each student's grade by identifying whether their mark falls within certain grade boundaries.

These types of decisions need the programmer to use **logical operators**. The basic logical operators supported by Python and their form in pseudocode are shown in Table 7.1:

Operator description	Pseudocode	Python 3
is equal to	=	==
is greater than	>	>
is less than	<	<
is greater than or equal to	>=	>=
is less than or equal to	<=	<=
is not equal to	!= or <>	!=

Table 7.1: Basic logical operators

KEY WORD

logical operators: allow programs to make a decision when comparing to conditions. They are sometimes called comparison operators. They include <, >, <=, >= and !=.

PRACTICE TASK 7.2

Double equals

Why does Python need to use a double equals sign as the logical 'equal to' operator, when pseudocode can use a single equals sign to represent the same operator?

7.3 Coding IF statements in Python

The code for an IF statement in Python is slightly different to that required in pseudocode. The Python programming language is designed to encourage programmers to write code that is easy to read. Indentation of four spaces is required and implemented by our IDEs to all blocks of code. A block of code in Python comes after a colon. All the lines of code that belong to this block are indented four spaces more than the line of code that ends with the colon. You can see how this works in the Python code below:

```python
number1 = int(input('Enter first number: '))
number2 = int(input('Enter second number: '))
if number2 == number1:
    print('Same')
else:
    if number2 > number1:
        print('Second')
    else:
        print('First')
```

Code snippet 7.3

TIP

Choosing correct logical operators is important. Using the wrong one can produce unexpected results in our algorithms. For example, it is very easy to choose > (for example, >60, which doesn't include 60) when >= (for example, >= 60, which does include 60) should be used. When trying out your programs, it is a good idea to test that they make the correct decisions at the boundaries.

This means that ending statements with semi-colons, wrapping code blocks in curly brackets, and adding ENDIF statements – which are needed in other programming languages – are all unnecessary. Note that, unlike in pseudocode, a colon is used on the previous line before indenting a block of code.

Compare the following pseudocode with its Python implementation.

Pseudocode:

```
discount ← 0.5
child ← TRUE
INPUT ticket_price


IF child = TRUE
  THEN
     ticket_price ← ticket_price * discount
ENDIF


OUTPUT ticket_price
```

Code snippet 7.4

Python code:

```
discount = 0.5
ticket_price = input('ticket price: ')

if child == True:
    ticket_price = ticket_price * discount

print(ticket_price)
```

Code snippet 7.5

DEMO TASK 7.1

Sort two numbers

Design a program that will input two whole numbers. If the second number is larger than the first, the program will output 'Second'; if not, the output should be 'First'.

Solution

First, we must produce the algorithm in either a flowchart or pseudocode. Because the task is phrased logically, this almost becomes a translation task:

```
INPUT number1, number2

IF number2 > number1
  THEN
    OUTPUT 'Second'
  ELSE
    OUTPUT 'First'
ENDIF
```

Code snippet 7.6

CONTINUED

Further Information: if ... elif ... else in Python

if statements in Python always begin with an if clause. However, we may wish to make other tests which may result in other outcomes. To do this we can add as many elif clauses as required. elif is short for "else if". We can also add else at the end of the sequence to do something different if all of the previous tests fail.

```
if <first test>:
    # do something
elif <second test>:
    # do something else
else:
    # do something different if other tests fail
```

Code snippet 7.7

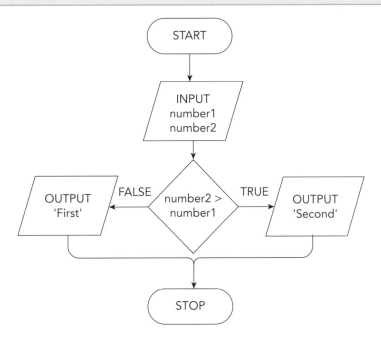

Flowchart 7.2

Having done this, we can use our preferred version of the algorithm as an outline for our Python program. With selection, this is easiest from pseudocode but neither of the algorithm representations are that difficult to write Python code from. Compare the Python code below (Code snippet 7.8) with the pseudocode algorithm shown in the Code snippet 7.6 and Flowchart 7.2:

```
number1 = int(input('Enter first number: '))
number2 = int(input('Enter second number: '))
if number2 > number1:
    print('Second')
else:
    print('First')
```

Code snippet 7.8

PRACTICE TASKS 7.3–7.6

7.3 Same as

a In Demo Task 7.1, what will happen if the same number is input twice?

b Demo Task 7.1 is re-worded: 'Design a program that will input two whole numbers. If the second number is the same or larger than the first, the program will output "Second"; if not the output should be "First".'

How would you change the algorithm to meet this change?

7.4 Match

a Draw a flowchart and write the pseudocode for a program that inputs two numbers. If the numbers are the same, the system outputs 'Match'. If the numbers are different, the system outputs 'No Match'.

b Write a text-based Python implementation of your algorithm in **a**.

7.5 Too large

a Draw a flowchart and write the pseudocode for a program that inputs two numbers. If the second number is more than twice the value of the first number, the system outputs 'Too Large' otherwise the system outputs 'Acceptable'.

b Write a text-based Python implementation of your algorithm in **a**.

7.6 Factor

a Draw a flowchart and write the pseudocode for a program that inputs two integers. If the second number is a factor of the first number, the system outputs 'Factor' otherwise the system outputs 'Not a Factor'.

b Write a text-based Python implementation of your algorithm in **a**.

> **TIP**
>
> For Task 7.5b, a factor of a number is any value that will divide exactly into that number.
>
> For example, the factors of 30 are 1, 2, 3, 5, 6, 10, 15 and 30.

Note: GUI applications are optional. They are not covered in the syllabuses.

CHALLENGE TASK 7.2

GUI versions

Choose two of the programs you wrote for Practice Tasks 7.4, 7.5 and 7.6. Then write new versions with a GUI interface. You will need two text boxes for the user to enter their two numbers, a label to display the message and a Submit button. A clear button might be useful too.

7.4 Multiple IF statements

Decisions do not always have to be made between two alternatives. Consider a program that takes as inputs two numbers and then outputs 'First', 'Second' or 'Same'. In this situation, we have three decisions to make. Problems like these can be solved by a series of IF statements, each of which ends before the following one starts, as shown in the following pseudocode and Python code.

Python code:

```
number1 = int(input('Enter first number: '))
number2 = int(input('Enter second number: '))

if number2 == number1:
    print('Same')

if number2 > number1:
    print('Second')

if number2 < number1:
    print('First')
```

Code snippet 7.9

Pseudocode:

```
INPUT number1
INPUT number2

IF number2 = number1
    THEN
        OUTPUT 'Same'
ENDIF

IF number2 > number1
    THEN
        OUTPUT 'Second'
ENDIF

IF number2 < number1
    THEN
        OUTPUT 'First'
ENDIF
```

Code snippet 7.10

Although this approach achieves the required outcome, it is inefficient. Consider the situation where both numbers are equal. The first IF statement would have produced the appropriate output, but even though the conditions in the following IF statements are false, the code must still execute them even if nothing is output to the screen. The algorithm produces the required output, but two IF statements have been executed unnecessarily.

PRACTICE TASK 7.7

First second same

Draw a flowchart version of the algorithm shown in Code snippets 7.9 and 7.10.

7.5 Nested IF statements

To avoid the inefficiency of several IF statements, it is possible to place one or more IF statements entirely within another. Each of the following IF statements will be executed only if the first condition proves to be false. These are known as **nested IF** statements.

The following pseudocode and Python code shows how a nested IF approach could be used instead of the inefficient sequence of IF statements shown in Section 7.4. Because the second IF statement will only execute if the criteria in the first statement is False, this avoids unnecessary execution of IF statements.

> **KEY WORD**
>
> **nested IF:** an IF statement with the ability for additional conditions to be checked once earlier conditions have determined a path.

Python code:

```
number1 = int(input('Enter first number: '))
number2 = int(input('Enter second number: '))

if number2 == number1:
    print('Same')
else:
    if number2 > number1:
        print('Second')
    else:
        print('First')
```

Code snippet 7.11

Pseudocode:

```
INPUT number1
INPUT number2

IF number2 = number1
    THEN
        OUTPUT 'Same'
    ELSE
        IF number2 > number1
            THEN
                OUTPUT 'Second'
            ELSE
                OUTPUT 'First'
        ENDIF
ENDIF
```

Code snippet 7.12

Notice how the colon in Python replaces the THEN in the pseudocode and that there is no need to have an ENDIF statement. When writing pseudocode in Cambridge IGCSE and O Level Computer Science papers, it is very important to include ENDIF clauses in pseudocode.

PRACTICE TASK 7.8

Many discounts

a   Write a flowchart and a pseudocode algorithm for a system that calculates the cost of a bus ticket. Your system must input the price of the ticket and the age of the passenger. Your system must output the final cost of the ticket using the information in the table below.

Age of Passenger	Discount	Final Ticket Price
Age 18 or above	No discount	Full price is charged.
Age 15 or above but less than 18	20% discount	Ticket is charged at 80% of full price.
Age 4 or above but less than 15	40% discount	Ticket is charged at 60% of the full price.
Aged under 4	100% discount	No charge, ticket is free.

b   Using nested IF statements, produce a text-based Python implementation and test that your algorithm works with a variety of inputs.

7.6 CASE statements

CASE statements are considered an efficient alternative to multiple IF statements where many choices depend on the value of a single variable.

KEY WORD

CASE statements: a simple method of providing multiple paths through the code based on a single variable or user input.

DEMO TASK 7.2

Different paths

Write a program where a user must input A, B or C. The code in your program must follow different paths depending on which letter has been input. Write two pseudocode algorithms for your program:

a   *Give an algorithm that uses nested IF statements.*

b   *Give an algorithm that uses CASE statements.*

Solution

The pseudocode in **a** shows the approach that would be taken using nested IF statements and **b** shows a CASE statement.

a

```
IF user_input = 'A'
  THEN
    // Code to follow
  ELSE
    IF user_input = 'B'
      THEN
        // Code to follow
      ELSE
        IF user_input = 'C'
          THEN
            // Code to follow
          ELSE
            OUTPUT 'Incorrect input'
        ENDIF
    ENDIF
ENDIF
```

Code snippet 7.13

b

```
CASE user_input
    'A':  // Code to follow
    'B':  // Code to follow
    'C':  // Code to follow
    OTHERWISE OUTPUT 'Incorrect input'
ENDCASE
```

Code snippet 7.14

Both approaches achieve the same outcome but the CASE statement is simpler to code and easier to read than the NESTED IF.

However, CASE statements are not available in Python.

Coding CASE statements in Python

There are IF statements in Python and there is the possibility to have nested IF statements, but there is no facility to write CASE statements. However, Python does provide us with a structure that is easier to read than nested IF statements and more flexible than CASE statements. Instead of a series of nested IF statements, Python programmers would use elif (short for ELSE IF).

This is how the pseudocode in Demo Task 7.2 would look in Python:

```python
user_input = input('Enter A,B or C: ')
if user_input == 'A':
    # code to follow
elif user_input == 'B':
    # code to follow
elif user_input == 'C':
    # code to follow
else:
    print('Incorrect Input')
```

Code snippet 7.15

When trying out pseudocode CASE solutions in Python, use the `if...elif...else` construct.

PRACTICE TASKS 7.9–7.10

7.9 Days in a month

a   Produce a flowchart or a pseudocode design of an algorithm for a program that inputs the name of a month and outputs the number of days in that month. Assume February will output 28 days.

> **Note:** GUI applications are optional. They are not covered in the syllabuses.

b   Write either a text-based or GUI implementation of your algorithm.

7.10 Leap year

a   Produce a flowchart or a pseudocode design of an algorithm for a program that will calculate if a person was born on a leap year. Your system must input the year of the person's birth and output either 'Leap Year' or 'Normal Year'.

The process for identifying if a year is a leap year:

Step 1   If the year is evenly divisible by 4 then go to step 2, otherwise go to step 5.

Step 2   If the year is evenly divisible by 100 then go to step 3, otherwise go to step 4.

Step 3   If the year is evenly divisible by 400 then go to step 4, otherwise go to step 5.

CONTINUED

Step 4   The year is a leap year and has 366 days.

Step 5   The year is not a leap year and has 365 days.

> **Note:** GUI applications are optional. They are not covered in the syllabuses.

b   Write either a text-based or GUI implementation of your algorithm.

CHALLENGE TASK 7.3

Efficiency and flexibility

Points for discussion:

a   You know that CASE statements are more efficient than a series of IF statements. Is a sequence of `elif` statements just as efficient as CASE statements?

b   How are Python's `elif` statements more flexible than CASE statements?

7.7 Drawing flowcharts for CASE statements

CASE statements are the most efficient code structure we have met for choosing different outcomes based on the value of a single variable. This is because they use the value as an index and go straight to that line of code, ignoring all others (see Flowchart 7.3(b)). Python's if...elif...else construct requires each evaluation to be made until the correct one is reached (and then the rest are skipped). This is the same situation as for nested IF statements.

The flowchart for nested IF statements and the Python solution are thus the same. The flowchart for the pseudocode in Demo Task 7.2 (Code snippet 7.13) can be seen in Flowchart 7.3(a). The pseudocode in Demo Task 7.2 (Code snippet 7.14) for the solution using CASE statements is better represented by the flowchart in Flowchart 7.3(b).

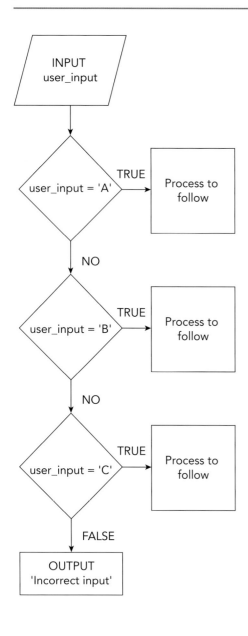

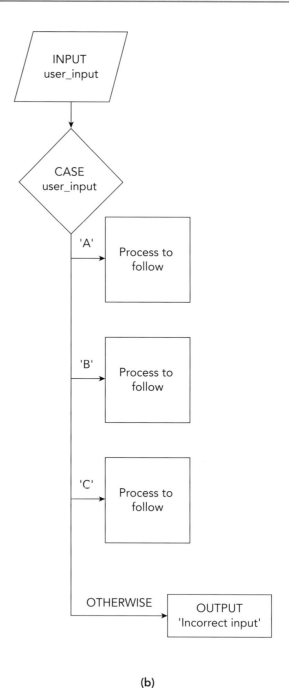

(a)

Flowchart 7.3: A nested IF example

(b)

Flowchart 7.3: A CASE example

7.8 Boolean operators

Often, a single logical operator is not sufficient to define the required criteria. For example, a fire alarm system may be required to activate if it detects either smoke or a high temperature. The logical operator in this case requires two criteria, either of which being true would cause the alarm to go off.

Python, in common with many other languages, uses the **Boolean operators** shown in Table 7.2:

> **KEY WORD**
>
> **Boolean operators:** The operators AND, OR and NOT allow a program to make a decision based on more than one condition.

Operator	Description	Example in Python
AND	**All** connected operators must be True for the condition to be met.	`if student_user == True and ID_number > 600:` The condition will only be `True` where the user is a student with an ID number higher than 600. Any other type of user with an ID number > 600 will not meet the criteria because it will fail the `student_user == True/` element of the condition.
OR	**Only one** of the connected conditions needs to be True for the condition to be met.	`if smoke_detected == True or temperature > 70:` The condition will be True if *either* smoke is detected *or* the temperature is above 70°C. It will also be True if both elements are met.

NOT	Used where it is easier to define the logical criteria in a negative way.	`if not input_number == 6:`
		
		The condition will be True for any number input with the exception of the number 6.
		
		Could also have been written:
		
		`if input_number != 6:`

Table 7.2: Boolean operators

Using AND to provide range criteria

In the following code, the condition is met if the input number is greater than 10 but less than 15.

```
if num > 10 and num < 15:
    # code to execute
```

Code snippet 7.16

Beware of getting the wrong Boolean operator. Using `or` in the statement would evaluate to True for any number.

> **TIP**
>
> It is very important to carefully check whether you should use OR or AND in your logic conditions. Sometimes when we use these words in conversation, the opposite Boolean operator is required in our programs.

Using the AND operator to replace a nested IF statement

A nested IF statement is often used to check two conditions.

```
if student_user == True:
    if ID_number > 600:
        # code to execute
```

Code snippet 7.17

When the conditions are simple, the nested IF statement can be replaced by AND. The following code represents the same conditions:

```
if student_user == True and ID_number > 600:
    # code to execute
```

Code snippet 7.18

Using logical connectors

In flowcharts, we need to be able to represent logical operators. We do this by using Boolean operators in the decision diamond.

Flowchart 7.4 represents Code snippet 7.17. Flowchart 7.5 represents Code snippet 7.18.

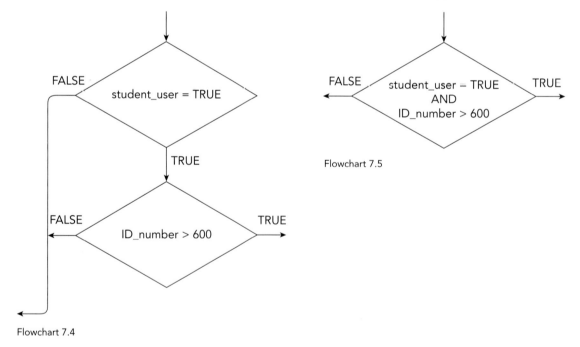

Flowchart 7.5

Flowchart 7.4

PRACTICE TASK 7.11

Leap year II

Look back at your Python solution for Practice Task 7.10. Using logical operators, rewrite it so that it only uses one `if` and one `else` clause.

SUMMARY

Selection allows algorithms to flow down different paths depending on the data being provided at the time.
The flowchart symbol for selection is a decision diamond. The alternative paths are indicated as True and False.
Logical operators, sometimes referred to as comparison operators, can provide the ability to program a range of outcomes. These include <, >, <=, >= and !=.
Boolean operators such as AND, OR and NOT can be used to link more than one condition together enabling programs to make complex decisions.
IF statements allow programs to provide different outcomes dependent on multiple variables or user inputs.
A string of separate IF statements can usually be replaced by more efficient nested IFs or CASE statements.
Nested IF statements allow programs to check additional conditions once a path has been determined by earlier conditions.
CASE statements can provide multiple paths based on a single variable or user input. They are not available in Python and should be replaced with `if ... elif ... else`.
The ELSE statement (used with IF) and the OTHERWISE statement (used with CASE) provide a default path should none of the conditions be met.

END-OF-CHAPTER TASKS

1 a Using either a flowchart or pseudocode, design an algorithm for a program that inputs three different integer values. The program will output the highest value input. If any of the integer values match, the program will output an error message.

b Write a text-based implementation using a NESTED IF solution.

c Write a text-based implementation using an ELSE IF solution.

2 a Using either a flowchart or pseudocode, design an algorithm for a system that calculates the cost of a ticket for a UK train. The train is based in London and only travels to two other locations in the UK. The train offers both economy and business class tickets. Details of the train costs are shown in the table.

A Return ticket allows a passenger to travel to a destination and back again.

Location / Extras	Economy		Business Class	
Edinburgh	One way	£32	One way	£87
	Return	£52	Return	£178
Cardiff	One way	£36	One way	£72
	Return	£50	Return	£138
On-board meal	One way	£12	Included in the price	
	Return	£18		

The program must obtain all the required information from the passenger before outputting the total cost of the ticket selected.

b Write a text-based Python implementation of your algorithm.

Note: GUI applications are optional. They are not covered in the syllabuses.

c Build a GUI version of the program you produced in **b**.

## Chapter 8

Iteration

IN THIS CHAPTER YOU WILL:

- use iteration in your programs

- design and represent iteration using flowcharts and pseudocode

- write code that will repeat instructions a number of times

- write code that will repeat instructions based on user input

- use counters with repeated code

- learn about the advantages and disadvantages of FOR, WHILE and REPEAT...UNTIL loops.

Introduction

There are many processes in life and programming that involve repetition. For example, we clean our teeth at the same time each day. Some medicines require us to shake the bottle a number of times before taking a dose. You have already come across a number of programs where you have repeated the same code several times – such as when you drew a square with a turtle robot. Rather than copying and pasting the same code several times, it is more efficient to put that code into what is called a loop. This makes our code shorter and easier to fix or amend if we need to.

8.1 Types of iteration

Three basic forms of iteration (Table 8.1) exist in the majority of programming languages. They are known as 'loops', because they cause the program to repeatedly 'loop through' the same lines of code.

Loop type	Description	When it should be used
FOR loop	Repeats a section of code a predetermined number of times.	The number of iterations is known. The programmer can set the code to loop the correct number of times.
WHILE loop	Repeats a section of code while the control condition is true.	The number of iterations is not known and it may be possible that the code will never be required to run. The condition is checked *before* the code is executed. If the condition is false, the code in the loop will not be executed.
REPEAT UNTIL loop	Repeats a section of code until the control condition is true.	The number of iterations is not known but the code in the loop must be run at least once. The condition is checked *after* the code has been executed, so the code will run at least once.

Table 8.1: The three basic loops

Often, it is possible to use any of the three types when producing an algorithm; however, each type offers the programmer certain advantages. Selecting the most appropriate type of loop can help to make your code more efficient.

8.2 FOR loops

A FOR loop can only be used where the number of iterations is known. It is traditional to use a variable named i (an abbreviation for the word 'index') as the loop counter.

Here are the pseudocode and Python syntax for a FOR loop:

Pseudocode:

```
FOR i ← 1 TO 10
    // Code to execute
NEXT
```

Code snippet 8.1

Python code:

```
for i in range(1,11):
    # Code to execute
```

Code snippet 8.2

Notice how neither the pseudocode nor the Python code needs to increment i within the loop; this is handled automatically by FOR loops. Do not forget, however, to add a line such as i = i + 1 to your flowcharts.

Let's look at the pseudocode (Code snippet 8.1) in more detail. Each individual element of the loop performs an important role in achieving the iteration, as shown in Table 8.2:

Element	Description
`FOR`	The start of the loop.
`i ← 1 TO 10`	i is a counter variable that records the number of iterations that have been run. This is usually increased by 1 every iteration. The value of the counter variable can be used within the loop to perform calculations.
`NEXT`	The end of the iteration section. The value of the counter variable is increased and the program goes back to the FOR line. The loop will check if the counter value is still within the condition (10 in this example). If the counter has exceeded the end value, the program will jump to the line of code after NEXT, if not the program will rerun the loop.

Table 8.2: Individual elements of a FOR loop

Now let's look at the Python code (Code snippet 8.2) in more detail. The code that is placed within the FOR loop will be repeated on each iteration. The block of code indented after the colon is all contained within the loop. In Python we use the range() function to control the FOR loop. In the example in Code snippet 8.2 the 1 is the starting number and 11 is the stop number. Try this out in the following short interactive session:

INTERACTIVE SESSION

Type the following code into the Python shell and then press return:

```
>>> for i in range(1,11):
        print(i)
```

Now find out what the following code does:

```
>>> for i in range(1,11):
        print(2*i)
```

Further Information:

Look again at the pseudocode:

```
FOR i ← 1 TO 10
    // Code to execute
NEXT
```

Code snippet 8.3

As the conditions are checked in the FOR line, NEXT always passes execution of the loop back to FOR to check the conditions. It is a common misconception that once the maximum number of iterations has been reached, NEXT will exit the loop. This is not true. Consider a situation where a FOR loop is written to execute ten times. Although the loop counter may have reached 10, NEXT will still increment the counter to 11 before passing execution to FOR. The value of the loop counter will then be outside of the condition and FOR will then exit the loop.

The Python code is somewhat different to the pseudocode:

```
for i in range(1,11):
    print(i)
```

Code snippet 8.4

Just as there are several types of loops in different languages, there are also different types of FOR loop. Python FOR loops are optimised for container variables. (You will learn about these in Chapter 10). There is no counter-controlled FOR loop in Python. Instead, the FOR loop in Python iterates through a group of variables and finds out for itself how many items there are in that group. This is very powerful.

However, to provide an implementation that is similar to the pseudocode style FOR loop that is used in the syllabuses, we need to use the `range()` function to generate a group of numbers.

`range()` takes three arguments:

- the integer to start at (default = 0)

- the first integer to exclude (required)

- the amount to increment by (default = 1).

Study the interactive sessions below to see how `range()` produces sequences of numbers. Note that the `list()` function is used to cast the sequence produced into a form that can be seen in the Python shell. (You will learn about lists in Chapter 10.)

INTERACTIVE SESSION

Create a sequence of numbers starting at 3 and ending before 10 in increments of 2:

```
>>> list(range(3, 10, 2))
[3, 5, 7, 9]
```

Create a sequence of numbers starting at 3 and ending before 10 in increments of 1:

```
>>> list(range(3, 10))  # if left out, the default increment is 1
[3, 4, 5, 6, 7, 8, 9]
```

Create a sequence of numbers starting at 0 and ending before 10 in increments of 1:

```
>>> list(range(10))  # if left out, the default start is 0
[0, 1, 2, 3, 4, 5, 6, 7, 8, 9]
```

(continued)

To produce a sequence of numbers from 1 to 10, we call `range(1,11)`. Therefore,

```
for i in range(1,11):
```

can be read as, 'For all items in the sequence [1, 2, 3, 4, 5, 6, 7, 8, 9, 10], loop through once and refer to the current item as i.'

In Python, if we need a loop that loops 10 times but we do not intend to use the index, we can simply write:

```
for _ in range(10):
```

The underscore is used in place of `i` to indicate that there is no intention to use the counter in the loop.

It is now much quicker to write a turtle program that draws a square:

```
# square.py
from turtle import *

for _ in range(4):
    forward(100)
    left(90)
```

Code snippet 8.5

PRACTICE TASKS 8.1–8.2

8.1 Turtle hexagon

Write a turtle program that uses a FOR loop and draws a hexagon with sides of length 100.

8.2 Turtle squares

Write a turtle program that uses two FOR loops to produce the pattern shown in Figure 8.1, which is made from 6 squares with sides of length 100.

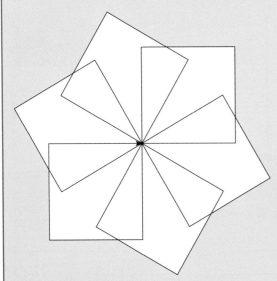

Figure 8.1: Turtle squares pattern

We will now learn how to design pseudocode and flowchart algorithms that use FOR loops.

Multiples

Write a program that outputs the multiples of a given number. Your program should stop after outputting ten multiples. For example, the multiples of 6 are 6, 12, 18, 24, 30, 36, 42, 48, 54 and 60.

Solution

Flowchart 8.1 shows the flowchart design of this algorithm. The pseudocode design is shown in Code snippet 8.6. Although this is quite easy to program, note how the flowchart is already quite complicated. This reflects the amount of work that is going on in a loop. Also, flowcharts show more clearly the detailed steps and will make it easier for us to see the difference between the three loop types.

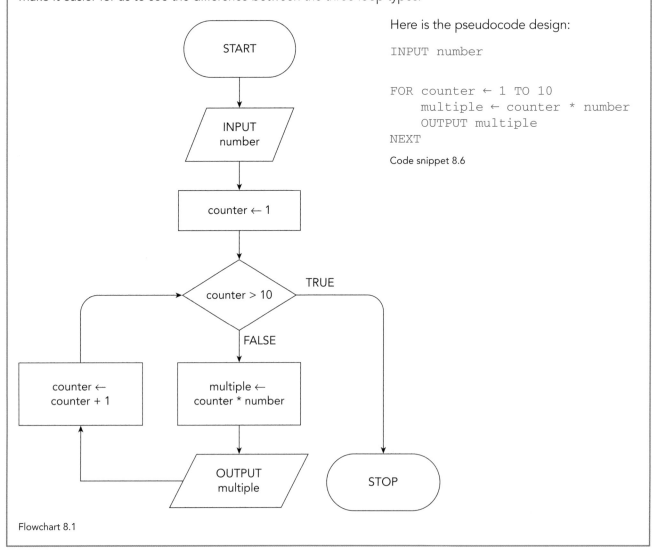

Here is the pseudocode design:

```
INPUT number

FOR counter ← 1 TO 10
    multiple ← counter * number
    OUTPUT multiple
NEXT
```

Code snippet 8.6

Flowchart 8.1

CONTINUED

The Python code for a text-based implementation of the algorithm shown in Flowchart 8.1 and Code snippet 8.6 is similar to the pseudocode, but we must remember to cast the user input from a string to an integer by wrapping the input statement in the `int()` function:

```python
# multiples.py
number = int(input('Input number to multiply: '))
for counter in range(1,11):
    multiple = number * counter
    print(multiple)
```

Code snippet 8.7

If the user enters 4, then the output from this program would be:

```
4
8
12
16
20
24
28
32
36
40
```

> **Note:** GUI applications are optional. They are not covered in the syllabuses.

A GUI application can also be made, as shown in Figure 8.2. This makes use of a text box that holds multiple lines of text. The layout has been achieved without using frames. The window size and colour have been provided by using tkinter's `geometry()` and `configure()` methods. A trick has been used to provide vertical spacing above the Output label.
When you look at the code, see if you can see how this was achieved.

Figure 8.2: GUI application of the Multiplier task

Items are added to the text box by using the code:

```
<Text box name>.insert(END, <string to add>)
```

The data to be added must be a String but as the result of the calculation is an Integer, it has to be cast with `str()` before it can be added to the text box. Here is the code to make the GUI program shown in Figure 8.2:

```python
# multiples-gui.py
from tkinter import *
def multiply():
    # get contents of textbox_input
    number = int(textbox_input.get())

    # clear output text box
    textbox_output.delete(0.0, END)
```

CONTINUED

```
    # process and output result
    for counter in range(1,11):
        multiple = str(number * counter) + '\n'
        textbox_output.insert(END, multiple)


# Build the GUI
window = Tk()
window.title('My App')


# give the window a size and background colour
window.geometry('150x350')
window.configure(background='linen')


# Create the labels
input_label = Label(window, text='Number: ', bg='linen')
input_label.grid(row=0, column=0)
output_label = Label(window, text='\nOutput: ', bg='linen')
output_label.grid(row=2, column=0)


# Create text entry box for entering number
textbox_input = Entry(window, width=5)
textbox_input.grid(row=1, column=0)


# Create text box for outputting multiples
textbox_output = Text(window, height=15, width=6)
textbox_output.grid(row=3, column=0)


# Create the button
multiply_button = Button(window, text='Get Multiples', command=multiply)
multiply_button.grid(row=1, column=1)


window.mainloop()
```

Code snippet 8.8

The trick to provide the vertical space above the label was to include a line return \n before the rest of the label text.

PRACTICE TASKS 8.3–8.4

8.3 Square numbers

a   Write a flowchart and pseudocode algorithm for a program that inputs an integer and outputs all the square numbers up to the square of the value of the input. (A square number is a number multiplied by itself. So, for example, if the input was 5 your program should output 1, 4, 9, 16, and 25.)

	1	2	3	4	5
Square	1	4	9	16	25

b   Write a Python implementation of your algorithm and test it works as expected.

8.4 Bit values

a   Write a flowchart and pseudocode algorithm for a program that inputs an integer and outputs that number of bit values of a binary number.

For example, if the input was 9, the output would be 1, 2, 4, 8, 16, 32, 64, 128, 256.

bit number	1	2	3	4	5	6	7	8	9
bit value	1	2	4	8	16	32	64	128	256

b   Write a Python implementation of your algorithm and test it works as expected.

TIP

For Task 8.4, note that each bit value is double the previous value.

8.3 WHILE loops

The WHILE...DO...ENDWHILE loop structure iterates while a condition is true.

The programmer may not know how many iterations this may generate. It is usual for the code within the loop to eventually produce a situation where the condition becomes false and the looping stops.

Because the conditions are tested at the start, it is possible that the loop will never run if the conditions are false at the outset. It is also possible to accidentally code an infinite loop where the conditions remain true forever.

KEY WORD

infinite loop: a type of iteration that has no termination condition and so goes on forever. This is sometimes created accidently by an error in a loop condition. There are also genuine uses, such as when an app has to always be listening for button presses.

When writing a **WHILE loop** in Python, you use the following format:

```
while counter > 0:
    # code to be iterated
    counter = counter - 1
```

Code snippet 8.9

This is very similar to the Cambridge IGCSE and O Level Computer Science pseudocode format:

```
WHILE counter > 0 DO
    // code to be iterated
    counter ← counter - 1
ENDWHILE
```

Code snippet 8.10

Each individual element of the loop in the Python code performs an important role, as shown in Table 8.3:

Element	Description
`while`	The start of the loop.
`counter > 0`	The condition that controls the loop. Each time the loop starts again, the condition is evaluated and, if it remains True, the code in the loop will run. Once the condition is False, execution of the code moves to the line of code following the loop. In counter-controlled WHILE loops, it is important that code is included within the loop to increment (increase) or decrement (decrease) the counter. In a FOR loop, the counter is automatically incremented. The same facility does not apply to WHILE loops and, as a result, the programmer must include appropriate code.
end of indented code	The end of the current iteration. Execution of the program returns to `WHILE` so the condition can be re-evaluated and further iterations take place. Do not forget to add ENDWHILE when writing pseudocode.

Table 8.3: Individual elements of a WHILE loop

> **TIP**
>
> Remember that WHILE loops iterate while the condition evaluates to True. It is possible to create an infinite loop rather easily:
>
> ```
> >>> while True:
>     print('Hello', end='')
> ```
>
> It is therefore important to know how to break out of infinite loops. To do so, hold down the **_CTRL_** key on your keyboard and press **_C_**. Try the code above yourself in an interactive session. The optional parameter `end=''` provided in the `print()` function suppresses the default line return.

KEY WORD

WHILE loop: a loop construct with a condition at the start of the loop to determine whether iteration should continue.

In Demo Task 8.1 (Multiples), we wrote a program that output the multiples of a given number up to a maximum of ten multiples. This can also be coded with a WHILE loop.

Compare Flowchart 8.2, and the pseudocode in Code snippet 8.11, with the FOR loop example in Flowchart 8.1 and Code snippet 8.6.

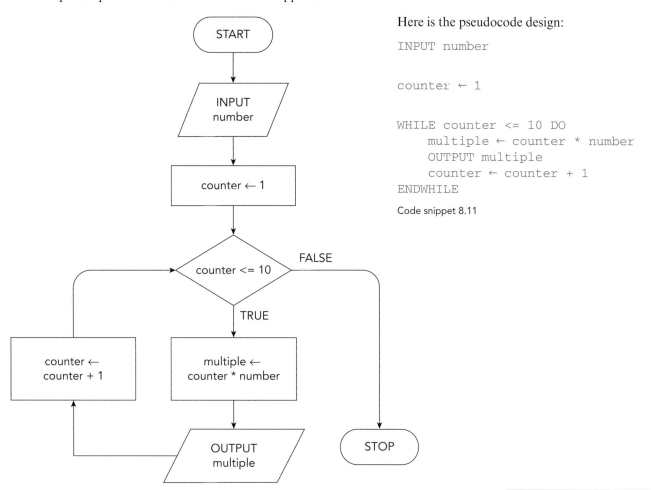

Here is the pseudocode design:

```
INPUT number

counter ← 1

WHILE counter <= 10 DO
     multiple ← counter * number
     OUTPUT multiple
     counter ← counter + 1
ENDWHILE
```

Code snippet 8.11

Flowchart 8.2

The flowcharts are nearly identical. A FOR loop uses **counting** to see if the counter has reached its target and, if it has not, keeps looping. A WHILE loop can evaluate any condition and keeps looping while the condition is True. Thus, when we add a counter and evaluate against that counter, it should not be a surprise that the flowcharts are similar. The only difference is that the logical condition is reversed in the flowchart:

FOR loop condition: counter <= 10

WHILE loop condition: counter >10.

> **KEY WORD**
>
> **counting:** a standard method of solution, used in programs that adds one for every item in a set of values to find out how many there are.

The format of the WHILE loop has been followed in the pseudocode. Note how the code block inside the loop includes a line that increases the counter by 1 each iteration.

The following is the code for a text-based Python implementation of the algorithm in Flowchart 8.2:

```
number = int(input('Input number to multiply: '))
counter = 1
while counter <= 10:
    multiple = number * counter
    print(multiple)
    counter = counter + 1
```

Code snippet 8.12

PRACTICE TASK 8.5

Nonsense sentences

Nonsense sentences is a game where a group of friends take turns to type a word each to generate a sentence. The first person starts with an adjective. The following players can keep adding adjectives or type a noun. After the noun is typed the next person types a verb and then there are more adjectives until another noun is typed. The following person must type in 'end'.

a   Design a flowchart algorithm for a program that inputs a series of words until 'end' is input and then outputs the nonsense sentence. As nonsense sentences is a game, your program can leave the players to follow the rules. No punctuation is required.

b   Write a Python text-based program that implements your algorithm.

c   Test your program with the following input: Yellow Jolly Chair Swallows Tasty Sand end

Note: GUI applications are optional. They are not covered in the syllabuses.

CHALLENGE TASK 8.1

Nonsense sentences GUI

See if you can design a GUI based Python version of the program you made in Practice Task 8.5b. It will be best if every time a word is submitted, you clear the text box ready for the next word.

Your button needs to be attached to a function that does this. Here is starter code for you:

```
#nonsense_sentences_gui.py
from tkinter import *
sentence = ''
```

CONTINUED

```
def submit_word():
    global sentence
    word = my_text_entry_box.get()

    if word != 'end':
        sentence = sentence + word + ' '
        my_text_entry_box.delete(0, END)
    else:
        output_label.config(text=sentence)
```

Notice how we are not using a loop in the function in this optional challenge. This is because the last line of your program will start tkinter's infinite loop:

```
window.mainloop()
```

Look at Appendix 2 if you need a reminder of where to put this line of code.

WHILE Loops with multiple criteria

While loops can have more complicated conditions applied than just counters. They can even continue to iterate until several conditions, linked by logical operators, evaluate to False. A simple example of this would be a login page. When a user gets either their username or password wrong, they must keep being asked to try again.

DEMO TASK 8.2

Login

Design a flowchart and pseudocode algorithm that repeatedly asks a user to enter their username and password while one or both of them is incorrect. Your program should let the user log in when they have got both the username and the password correct. Then provide a Python implementation to test your solution.

Solution

First let's think about the condition for our WHILE loop. It must evaluate to True while the user enters an incorrect username or password. This should do:

```
WHILE username is incorrect OR password is incorrect DO
```

CONTINUED

Flowchart 8.3 shows the flowchart for a complete solution and Code snippet 8.13 shows the pseudocode solution.

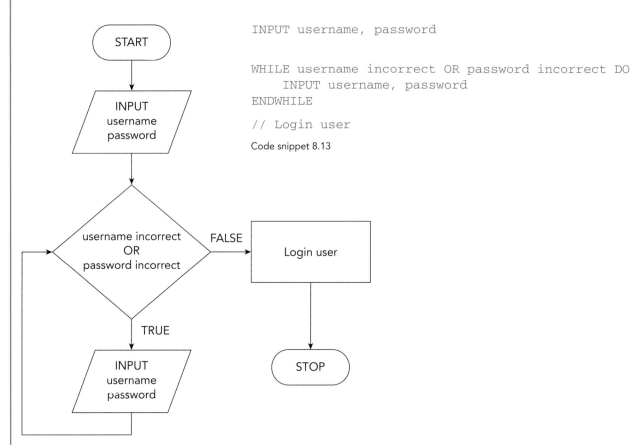

```
INPUT username, password

WHILE username incorrect OR password incorrect DO
      INPUT username, password
ENDWHILE
// Login user
```

Code snippet 8.13

Flowchart 8.3

To develop a text-based Python solution to this task, we first need to provide some test data. From then on, the program follows a familiar path: first we ask for user input and then we use the control condition from Code snippet 8.13 in a while loop. Below (Code snippet 8.14) is the code for a text-based implementation:

```python
# login.py
# Test data
correct_username = 'johnsmith'
correct_password = 'yellowbrickroad'


# Start program
username = input('Input your username: ')
password = input('Input your password: ')
```

```
while username != correct_username or password != correct_password:
    print('Error!')
    username = input('Input your username: ')
    password = input('Input your password: ')


print('Login successful.')
```
Code snippet 8.14

PRACTICE TASK 8.6

20 or fewer

a   Design a pseudocode and flowchart algorithm for a program that will calculate the average value from a series of positive integers input by the user. Your program should print out the answer after 20 values have been entered. Alternatively, a user can input −1 to indicate there are no more numbers to average. At either point, your program should output the average of the values input (excluding the final −1).

b   Write a Python implementation and test it works as expected.

8.4 REPEAT...UNTIL loops

A **REPEAT...UNTIL loop** is very similar to a WHILE loop as iteration will continue based on the loop conditions. It will therefore also work when the number of iterations is unknown.

Unlike in a WHILE loop, the test to check whether the condition is True or False is completed at the end of the iteration. This means that the code inside the loop will always run at least once.

There is no REPEAT...UNTIL loop in Python, but your algorithms can be implemented in Python by creating an infinite loop and then using `break` after testing at the end of the loop:

```
counter = 1
while True:
    # Code for iteration
    counter = counter + 1
    if counter > 10:
        break
```

Code snippet 8.15

The individual elements of the Python code perform an important role in the iteration, as shown in Table 8.4:

Element	Description
`while True`	The start of the loop. By replacing the normal condition that is required to evaluate to True with True, we ensure that this loop will continue forever. At every iteration, the execution of the program will be passed to the while True command. Because the loop starts before any conditions are checked, the iteration will always run at least once.
`break`	Stop looping.
`counter > 10`	The condition for the loop. Each time the loop is run, the condition is evaluated. If it remains False, the program continues from the `while True` line and the iteration will run again. Once the condition is True, the program leaves the loop and runs whatever code follows the loop. It is possible to use the logical operators (AND, OR and NOT) to structure multiple conditions. Counter-based conditions require the counter to be incremented by the code in the loop.

Table 8.4: Individual elements of the WHILE True loop

> **TIP**
>
> Because the check in a REPEAT...UNTIL loop is made at the end of the block of code, it is important to remember that the code in the loop will always run at least once.

DEMO TASK 8.3

Login 2

Construct a flowchart and pseudocode algorithm that asks a user to enter their username and password while one or both of them is incorrect. Your program must use a REPEAT...UNTIL loop and let the user log in when they have got both the username and the password correct. Then provide a Python implementation to test your solution.

Solution

The REPEAT...UNTIL loop is shown in Flowchart 8.4 and Code snippet 8.16. If you compare these with the WHILE approach in Flowchart 8.3 and Code snippet 8.13, you will be able to identify the differences in approach. The decision conditions are checked at different stages during the process: the WHILE at the outset of the loop and the REPEAT...UNTIL at the end. The loop decision for the WHILE is based on the criteria being True and the REPEAT...UNTIL loops if the conditions evaluate to False.

This task is a situation where the REPEAT...UNTIL loop is the better solution. We do not need to repeat our input code because our users were always going to want to try and login once. Testing whether the username and password are both correct feels more natural than testing whether one or other of them is incorrect.

CONTINUED

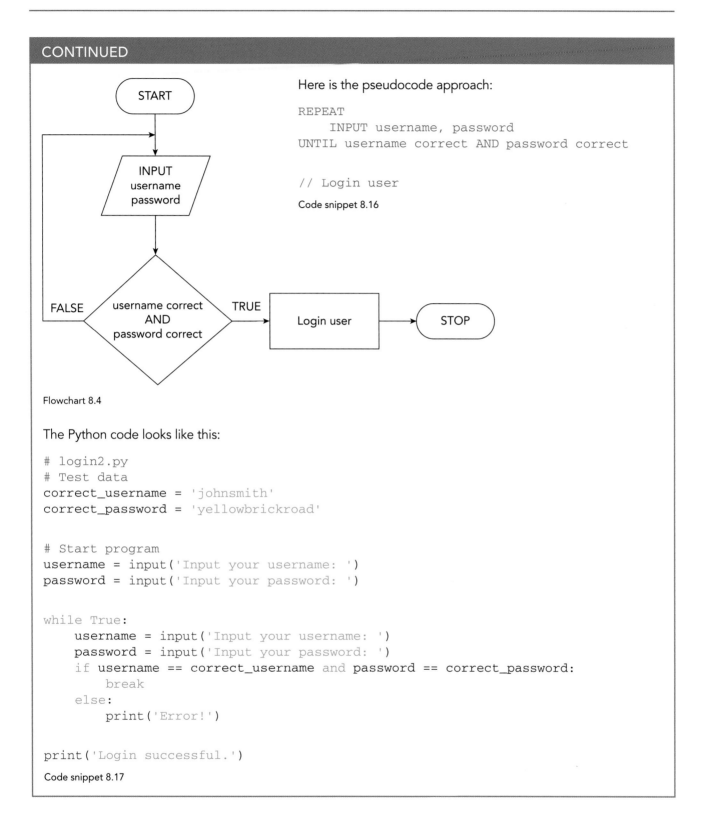

Here is the pseudocode approach:

```
REPEAT
    INPUT username, password
UNTIL username correct AND password correct

// Login user
```

Code snippet 8.16

Flowchart 8.4

The Python code looks like this:

```python
# login2.py
# Test data
correct_username = 'johnsmith'
correct_password = 'yellowbrickroad'

# Start program
username = input('Input your username: ')
password = input('Input your password: ')

while True:
    username = input('Input your username: ')
    password = input('Input your password: ')
    if username == correct_username and password == correct_password:
        break
    else:
        print('Error!')

print('Login successful.')
```

Code snippet 8.17

PRACTICE TASK 8.7

Choose a password

a   Construct a flowchart and pseudocode algorithm for a program that asks a user to enter their password twice. Your program must use a REPEAT... UNTIL loop. If the user has entered two identical passwords and the chosen password has more than ten characters, your program should output 'Password accepted' otherwise it should output 'Error!' and ask for the input again.

b   Write a Python implementation of your algorithm to test your solution.

8.5 Gathering experimental data

There are many experiments and surveys that can be carried out involving data gathering. Here is one such example.

A student wants to run an experiment that involves recording the height and age of all the students they meet. The data can be recorded using either a WHILE or REPEAT... UNTIL loop. As all the heights and ages are positive, it is possible to use a negative number to indicate when the data-gathering process is over. The control condition used to exit the loop can then be 'exit if the height entered is negative'.

In this scenario, the input would be placed within either a WHILE or a REPEAT... UNTIL loop. The loop condition would be based on the height input value. The algorithm to maintain the total number of records entered and the height averages would iterate in the loop. The output of the system could be programmed to display only when the loop had ended.

DEMO TASK 8.4

Summing user input

Write a program that will allow a user to input a series of positive numbers. The end of the sequence will be indicated by inputting a value of −1. Your program should then output the sum of the positive numbers input.

CONTINUED

Solution

The demo task chosen here is a simple one so we can produce and compare both a WHILE and a REPEAT...UNTIL loop solution. First let's draw a flowchart based on the description of what is required. The flowchart in Flowchart 8.5 does not show which of our two loop structures is to be used – it simply includes the condition in the loop.

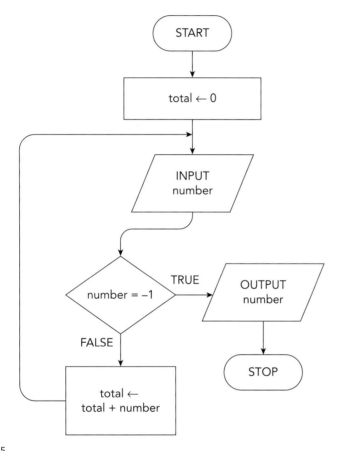

Flowchart 8.5

The different approaches can be seen in the pseudocode shown in Code snippets 8.18 and 8.19.

The WHILE loop in pseudocode Code snippet 8.18 requires the first number to be input outside the loop to provide a value to check.

The REPEAT...UNTIL loop in pseudocode Code snippet 8.19 includes the input of −1 for total as the conditions are not checked until after the processing in the loop has been completed. Consequently, the total has to be recalculated after the loop.

CONTINUED

```
total ← 0                        total ← 0
INPUT number
                                 REPEAT
WHILE number is not -1 DO             INPUT number
    total ← total + number           total ← total + number
    INPUT number                UNTIL number = -1
ENDWHILE                        total ← total + 1


OUTPUT total                    OUTPUT total
```

Code snippet 8.18   Code snippet 8.19

PRACTICE TASK 8.8

Summing user input

a   Write a text-based Python program using the pseudocode algorithm shown in Code snippet 8.18.

b   Write a text-based Python program using the pseudocode algorithm shown in Code snippet 8.19.

c   Test both of your programs to check that they produce the same results.

SKILLS FOCUS 8.1

WHICH CONDITION-CONTROLLED LOOP?

As we have seen, both loops can perform the same task. You are probably wondering when you would choose one of these two **condition-controlled loops** over the other?

To make this decision, we need to consider the key differences between the two loops – these are shown in Table 8.5:

Loop	Difference
WHILE	Will check conditions at the start of the loop. As a result, the block of code in the loop may not run.
REPEAT…UNTIL	Will check conditions at the end of loop. As a result, the block of code in the loop will always run at least once.

Table 8.5: Differences between WHILE and REPEAT…UNTIL loops

KEY WORD

condition-controlled loops: types of iteration where the repetition of the loop is determined by conditions. The number of times the loop will be executed is unknown.

CONTINUED

WHILE loops are most appropriate in programs where:

- An input is tested to decide if the process should iterate.

- A series of inputs are totalled or compared with an input value to end the loop. When the input is tested at the start of a loop, it avoids the end value being included in the totalling or comparison.

REPEAT...UNTIL loops are most appropriate in programs where:

- The process within the loop must run at least once.

- The criteria to be checked are generated within the loop.

For each of the following scenarios, say whether a WHILE loop or a REPEAT...UNTIL loop is likely to be the best solution.

Questions

1 A program used to calculate the total of a series of inputs. The series will end when a negative number is input.

2 A program used to stop a series of numerical inputs as soon as the total of those inputs is above 1000.

3 A program that allows a user to access a system if the username and password they input match the system records. Incorrect inputs will be rejected and users will be asked to try again.

KEY WORD

totalling: a standard method of solution, used in programs, that adds up multiple values to find the total.

SUMMARY

Iteration allows programmers to loop through blocks of code multiple times.
There are three main types of iteration: FOR, WHILE and REPEAT...UNTIL loops.
Flowcharts show loops with a decision diamond and a flow line looping back to an earlier element of the flowchart. The decision contains the conditions on which the iteration is based.
A FOR...TO...NEXT loop is used where the number of iterations is known at the outset.
Condition-controlled loop structures, such as WHILE...DO...ENDWHILE or REPEAT...UNTIL, are used where the number of iterations is unknown.
WHILE...DO...ENDWHILE structures check the loop conditions at the start of the loop. If the conditions are False, the loop will never run.
REPEAT...UNTIL structures check the loop conditions at the end of the first iteration. Consequently, the loop will always run at least once.
WHILE loops continue to iterate while the condition equates to True.
REPEAT...UNTIL loops continue iterating while the condition equates to False.
To implement a counting FOR loop in Python, the `range()` function is used.

END-OF-CHAPTER TASKS

1   What type of loop is the best choice for the following?

   a   A program used to output the average examination score of a class of 25 students.

   b   A program used to record the temperature of a chemical reaction. Temperatures will be recorded every minute. The last record will be made when the temperature has reached 20°C.

   c   A program used to record the times of 200 marathon runners.

   d   A program used in a cinema to record the age range of the people who watch a film. As each person buys a ticket, their age is entered into the system.

2   a   Design either a flowchart or pseudocode algorithm for a program that will input a positive integer. The program must then output all the factors of that number.

   b   Write a text-based Python implementation of your algorithm.

3   Write a turtle program that will input a positive integer from 3 to 10. Your program will then draw a regular polygon with the number of sides that were input.

4   Design and write a program that will input two positive integers and output all the common factors of the two numbers input.

5   Here is the Fibonacci series:

   0, 1, 1, 2, 3, 5, 8, 13, ...

   The series starts with the values 0 and 1. Each subsequent number is the sum of the previous two.

   a   Design a flowchart or pseudocode algorithm for a program that inputs an integer, n, and then outputs the first n numbers in the Fibonacci series.

   b   Write a Python implementation of your algorithm.

TIP

For Task 2a, a factor is a number that will divide into the provided number without a remainder.

TIP

For Task 3, you may want to do some research to find out what angles are needed to draw these shapes; however, it is smarter to calculate the angles required in your program.

TIP

For Task 4, your program should loop to find if a value is a factor of the first number and then check if the value is also a factor of the second number. Only if the value divides into both numbers without a remainder will it be a common factor.

> Chapter 9
System design

IN THIS CHAPTER YOU WILL:

- learn that systems are made up of subsystems, which may in turn be made up of further subsystems

- understand how to apply top-down design and structure diagrams to simplify a complex system

- combine sequence, selection and iteration to design complex systems

- understand how to produce effective and efficient solutions to complex tasks.

Introduction

When designing algorithms, you will make use of computational thinking. This requires the ability to analyse a scenario-based task, identify the individual elements of the task and use programming concepts to create an appropriate algorithm. Often, more than one approach to a given scenario will produce a working solution, which makes this process exciting. Identifying and designing an efficient solution to a problem is at the heart of computational thinking.

9.1 Top-down design

Top-down design breaks a large problem into simple steps or tasks. Each of these tasks may be split into a number of smaller subtasks. The process is complete once the problem has been broken down sufficiently to allow it to be understood and programmed. This process is also known as 'step-wise refinement'.

The main advantage of designing solutions in this way is that the final process will be well structured and easier to understand. It can increase the speed of development as different subtasks can be given to individual members of a programming team. This design approach also helps when debugging or modifying programs. Changes can be made to individual subtasks without necessarily having to change the overall program.

This approach is effective in solving large, real-world problems as well as the type of scenario-based questions you may meet during an examination.

> **Further Information:**
>
> Top-down design is not the only way of solving large real-world problems. Object-oriented programming also involves breaking up large problems into smaller parts. A complex system is examined to see what objects the system is made of and then these are built and put together to recreate the whole system. Breaking up complex problems into smaller more manageable parts is an important computational thinking skill called decomposition. These syllabuses focus on top-down design.

9.2 Structure diagrams

One tool available to programmers when trying to design a solution to a more complex system is the structure diagram. When using top-down design, the aim is to decompose the system into smaller and smaller problems until no further decomposition can take place. At this point, the programmer can develop algorithms for each sub-problem in the usual way, using flowcharts or pseudocode.

KEY WORDS

top-down design: a way of designing a computer program by breaking down the problem into smaller problems (subsystems) until it is sufficiently defined to allow it to be understood and programmed. This is sometimes known as step-wise refinement.

structure diagrams: a method of expressing a system as a series of subsystems using a diagram.

decomposition: a computational thinking skill that involves thinking about large tasks and breaking them down into smaller tasks.

DEMO TASK 9.1

School register

A school requires a system that will check if students are present in lessons and report to parents any absence. The teacher will record if students are in the lesson and then transfer the record to the school administration team, who will contact parents if students are absent. Parents can be contacted either by telephone or email.

Produce a structure diagram for this system.

Solution

One possible strategy is to think about the situation in terms of the steps of a computer model:

Input → Storage → Process → Output

We could start the design by thinking about the main elements of the required system:

- The main input will be the record of the students' presence.

- To store this, some form of list could be used.

- We need to record the presence of every student who attends the lesson.

Figure 9.1 shows the initial structure diagram for this system:

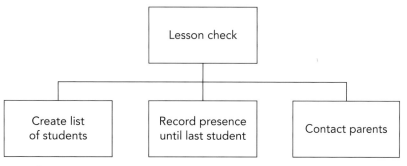

Figure 9.1: Initial structure diagram

The next step is to think about whether any of the tasks could be broken down into subtasks. 'Create List of Students' is a high-level task that could be broken down into subtasks. 'Contacting Parents' can be done by telephone or email and will therefore also need subtasks. Figure 9.2 shows the amended structure diagram with these subtasks.

CONTINUED

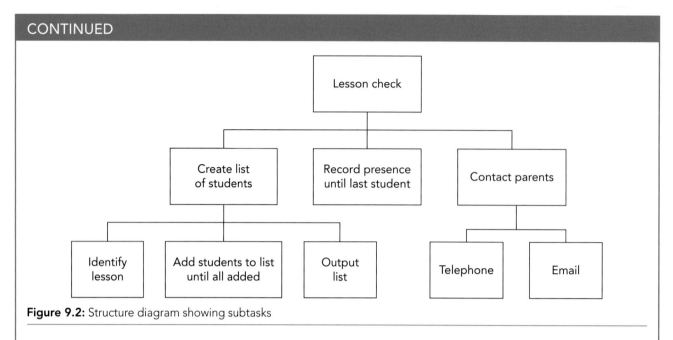

Figure 9.2: Structure diagram showing subtasks

The diagram may not yet be complete. The process 'Identify lesson' could be broken into further subtasks. What inputs would be needed? Where is the data about which students attend the lesson stored? How will the system access those records? These and other tasks would require consideration if this was a real-life scenario.

This process of breaking down each task is continued until all subtasks have been identified.

PRACTICE TASK 9.1

Weather app

A weather app works by using location data entered by the user. The user will choose either a new town or a previously saved town. The weather app will then output the day's forecast either as a visual map or a table of temperatures, windspeeds and weather icons.

A weather app is an example of a computer system that is made up of subsystems. The structure diagram (Figure 9.3) shows some of its subsystems. Complete the diagram by filling in the empty boxes.

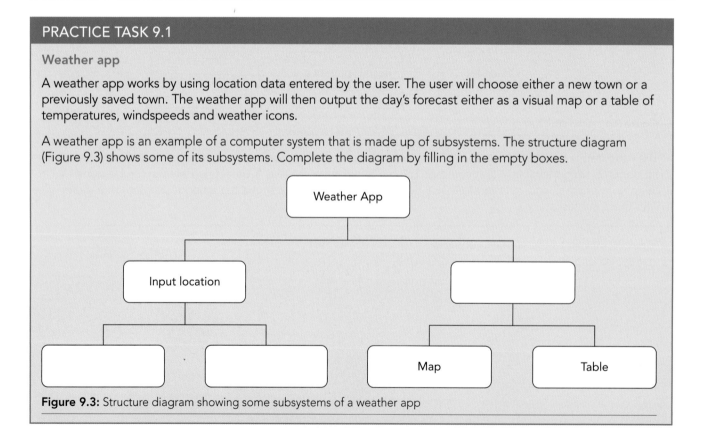

Figure 9.3: Structure diagram showing some subsystems of a weather app

9.3 Design steps

As suggested in Demo Task 9.1, splitting the overall task into subtasks can be done following the Input → Storage → Process → Output computer model.

When designing an algorithm for a subtask, it is recommended that a slight adaption is made to the process:

1   Identify the inputs and outputs that are involved in the scenario. At this stage, it is worth identifying any global variables that will be required.

2   For each input, identify if the task requires this input to be repeated. This will mean some form of iteration is needed. Identify the most appropriate loop to use.

3   For each output, identify the required calculation or recording process required to produce the output value.

   a   Does the process involve any decision making? This could mean use of an IF statement.

   b   Does the process involve repeated calculation? This could mean some form of iteration.

4   Consider the sequence in which the various processes need to be completed:

   •   Check that inputs or processes that need to be iterated are within the loop.

   •   Check that single inputs and outputs are outside the loop.

   •   Check that all iterations repeat as expected.

   •   Check that you have defined and initialised the variables or constants that are to be used.

Thinking about the inputs and outputs at the start will help you to consider the aim of the system. You will not be able to define the process required to produce the outputs if you do not identify the required outputs early in the design stage. Although variables are considered at the start, they can be finalised as a last step to making sure nothing has been missed.

> **TIP**
>
> When programming, your IDE will alert you to incorrect statements and missing variables. When designing in pseudocode, this support is not available. Always check that you have initialised all global variables correctly and that program statements are complete.

DEMO TASK 9.2

Known quantity of inputs

A user will input 100 positive numbers into a system. The system will output the highest number and the sum of the numbers input. Design an appropriate algorithm.

Solution

Figure 9.4 outlines the computational thinking process for designing the algorithm using the steps described above.

CONTINUED

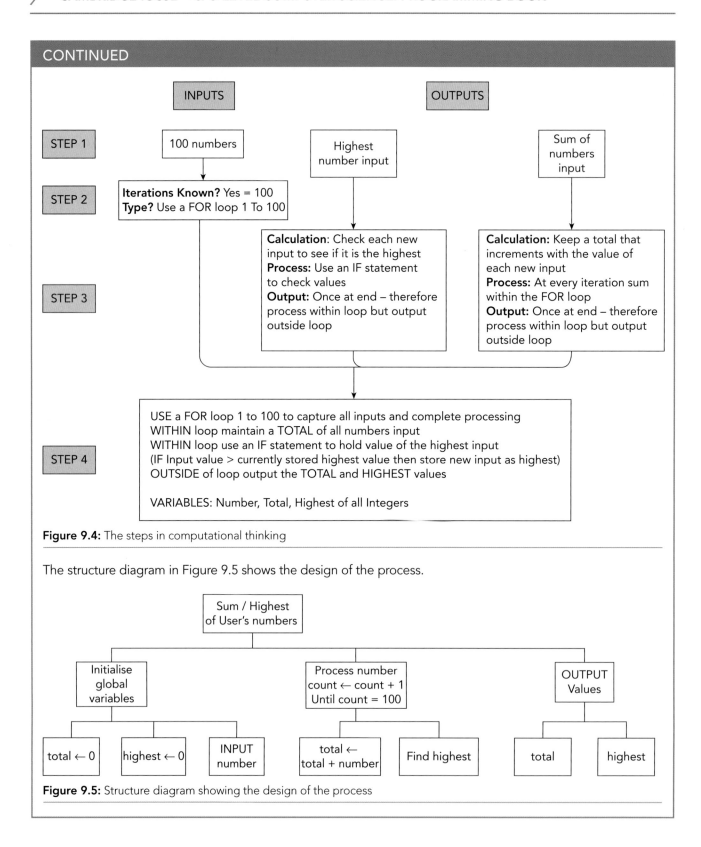

Figure 9.4: The steps in computational thinking

The structure diagram in Figure 9.5 shows the design of the process.

Figure 9.5: Structure diagram showing the design of the process

From this, we can produce Flowchart 9.1.

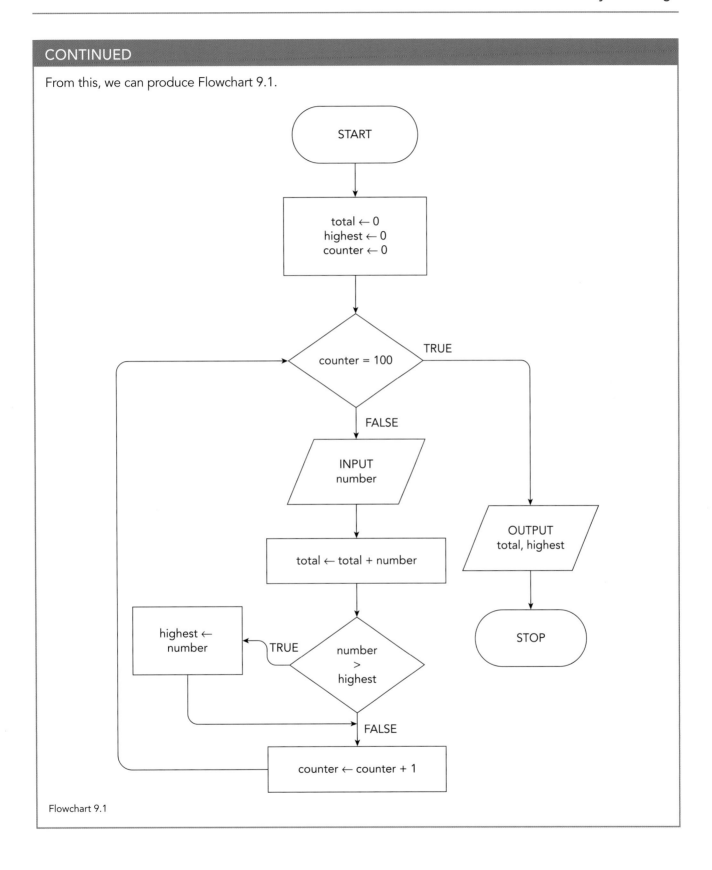

Flowchart 9.1

CONTINUED

Here is the pseudocode design:

```
total ← 0
highest ← 0

FOR counter = 1 TO 100
    INPUT number
    total ← total + number
    IF number > highest
      THEN
          highest ← number
    ENDIF
NEXT

OUTPUT total, highest
```
Code snippet 9.1

When finding the highest number in the algorithm above we are 'finding the **maximum**', one of the standard methods of solution. This involves initialising a variable, in this case `highest`, to a value lower than any to be entered. We then loop through all input values and compare them with `highest` updating this value whenever the new value is greater than the current value. To find the **minimum** in a set of numbers we use the same process, but first initialise a variable to a very large number.

KEY WORDS

maximum: the largest item in a set of data.

minimum: the smallest item in a set of data.

PRACTICE TASKS 9.2–9.3

9.2 Discussion question

The solution shown in Demo Task 9.2 is not the only acceptable solution. Identify two other ways this algorithm could have been written.

9.3 Design: Unknown quantity of inputs

A librarian is required to input the number of pages of each book in a set of books. The librarian will indicate the end of the input sequence by inputting a negative value. The system will output the average number of pages in the set of books.

a   Produce a structure diagram for this system.

b   Produce a flowchart for this system.

c   Produce a pseudocode algorithm for this system.

d   Write a Python implementation of your algorithm and test that it works.

TIP

To check that your solutions work as intended, they should be tested. See Chapter 12 to discover how this can be achieved.

CHALLENGE TASKS 9.1–9.2

9.1 Rainfall problem

A system is designed to collect monthly rainfall data in millimetres from weather stations around the UK. It then has to output a monthly rainfall figure for each location and the average for the whole country. Not all weather stations will fill in their data though. Draw a structure diagram that breaks this system down into subsystems. Note that there is more than one correct answer to this question.

9.2 Local rainfall

Local weather stations have been asked to enter the number of millimetres of rain falling in each day of the month when there is more than 0.1 mm of rain collected. There are therefore going to be a maximum of 31 entries and a minimum of 0 entries, but each station will enter a different number of data points. Design a program that will input a list of daily rainfall totals (to the nearest 0.1 mm), end when a negative number is entered and then output the total rainfall for the month. Produce your algorithm as a flowchart first and then write a Python implementation.

9.4 The complete design process

When presented with a complex problem, any or all of the following processes might be needed to create a finished solution:

- Decomposition – using top-down design and structure diagrams.
- Algorithms – using flow charts and pseudocode initially and then examining the algorithm to see if it could be simplified, or made more efficient by employing loops or subroutines.
- Check input data – this is called validating user input (see Chapter 11).
- Testing – thorough testing needs to then take place (see Chapter 12).

Simplifying algorithms makes for more reliable and maintainable solutions. Efficient algorithms use loops and functions to collect repetitive input and processing. An efficient algorithm will combine the collection of multiple processes in one loop rather than in separate loops wherever possible.

You are expected to be able to design effective solutions and comment on the effectiveness of algorithms presented to you. Remember to check whether the solution could be simplified further or made more efficient as well as whether it handles all your test data (Chapter 12), and that all input is effectively validated (Chapter 11). The efficiency of different solutions is examined in more depth in Chapter 8 where the use of different kinds of loops is compared, and again in Chapter 14 where advice is given on how to prepare for programming scenario-based tasks.

SUMMARY

Systems are made up of subsystems, which may in turn be made up of further subsystems.
Top-down design is a method of simplifying the main system into its subsystems until the whole system is sufficiently defined to allow it to be understood and programmed.
Structure diagrams are a diagrammatical method of describing a system as a series of subsystems.
When designing solutions for a given problem, using an Input → Storage → Process → Output approach can help to design an effective solution.
Flowcharts, pseudocode, top-down design, structure diagrams, simplification, efficiency analysis, validation and testing are used when designing programmed systems.
Effective solutions are ones that cannot be further simplified, are efficient, pass a testing regime and have effective validation of input.

END-OF-CHAPTER TASKS

1 Produce a system that inputs a list of monthly rainfall totals from weather stations produced by the system in Challenge Task 9.2. When the list ends, a −1 will be input to indicate there is no more data. Your program should then output the number of reporting weather stations and the average rainfall for the UK in that particular month. Produce your algorithm in pseudocode first and then write a Python implementation.

2 A game involves toys randomly popping up out of a set of holes. The player has to hit as many as possible with a soft toy mallet in a minute. A system is required that inputs a 1 for each successful hit. When the minute is up, the total score is output. For the purpose of this exercise, your program should input a number of consecutive 1s (up to 100) and −1 to indicate the time is up.

a Design a flowchart to describe this system and then a Python implementation.

Note: GUI applications are optional. They are not covered in the syllabuses.

b Design a GUI to simulate this. There should be a button that you can press with your mouse repeatedly to indicate successful hits. There should also be a second 'Finish' button that can be pressed when the time is up and the output is required. You will also need a textbox where the score can be output.

c If you are feeling very adventurous, you could try and write a program that gives a player 60 seconds and then outputs the score. You can try to produce a GUI with nine buttons which are randomly highlighted for a second or two and have to be selected with the mouse, while highlighted, to score. This is a difficult (and optional) challenge that will require you to use a number of the skills taught in this chapter to complete. You will probably also need to look up some more information online to find out how to change the background colour of tkinter buttons in Python. Note that no solution is provided and this is beyond the scope of the syllabuses!

CONTINUED

3   You have been asked to write a turtle program that can draw a house like the one shown here.

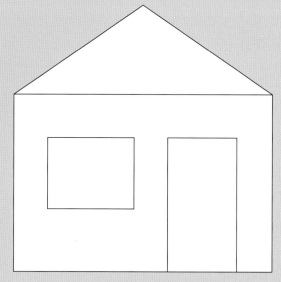

a   Draw a structure diagram that breaks this system down into subsystems – e.g. draw a rectangle, draw a triangle. Note there is more than one correct answer to this question.

b   Write algorithms for one of your subsystems as either a flowchart or in pseudocode.

c   Write a Python program that draws a house similar to the one shown.

TIP

For Task 3c, you will need to think about lifting and putting down the pen. You will probably want to use the turtle `goto()` command.

## Chapter 10

Arrays

IN THIS CHAPTER YOU WILL:

- learn how to define an array using flowcharts and pseudocode

- understand how to declare and use an array

- learn how to read from and write values to an array

- learn how to use a number of arrays to organise data

- understand how to use two-dimensional arrays

- use Python's list data type as a substitute for arrays when implementing your algorithms

- learn about linear searches and bubble sort.

Introduction

Before I go shopping, I often make a list of the items I want to get. If I were to write a program to simulate this, it would be a very tedious task if I had to declare and initialise a variable for each item in my shopping list. Thankfully, programmers can use arrays to store several items with the same data type, such as strings. Arrays only have to have one declaration and are then auto-indexed so each item in the list can easily be accessed.

An array is an example of a container data type. The standard Python library does not support arrays. If arrays are required, then the array built-in library must be imported first. The reason the standard library does not support arrays is because Python has a rich set of alternative container data types called tuples, lists and dictionaries. You will see later in this chapter that the Python version of the FOR loop is designed to work very closely with these container data types.

It is recommended that, when implementing your pseudocode and flowchart solutions in Python, you use lists to replicate arrays. A list can do everything an array can do and more. For example, lists are able to store a variety of data types at the same time and can be lengthened or shortened as required.

It is worth noting that although lists are more flexible than arrays, arrays are more efficient for most simple processes.

> **KEY WORD**
>
> container data type: a data type that can contain more than one data item (e.g. arrays and lists).

10.1 Declaring an array

Declaring an array is similar to the process of declaring a variable. The difference is that you need to define the size of the array. The size of an array is the number of data items that the array is required to hold. Each individual value held within an array is identified by an index number. Index numbers are sequential and, in Python, as with many other programming languages, the numbering starts from zero.

Table 10.1 is a diagrammatic representation of an array designed to hold the first five letters of the Greek alphabet.

> **KEY WORD**
>
> array: a data structure that can hold a set of data items of the same data type under a single identifier.

Index number	0	1	2	3	4
Data item	Alpha	Beta	Gamma	Delta	Epsilon

Table 10.1: Representation of an array

The pseudocode format for declaring an array capable of holding the five values is as follows. Note how the range of indices is 0 to 4:

```
greek_letter[0:4] OF String
```

Not all languages number array items from zero and you may see an example of arrays that start from 1. In this example, the final index would then become 5:

```
greek_letter[1:5] OF String
```

When writing pseudocode, either method of numbering is acceptable; however, it is vital to remain consistent when using arrays in algorithms. If the array is declared as [0:4] then the following pseudocode must also follow that format. That is, the first data item must be held in index 0 and the fifth data item in index 4.

The syntax for declaring a **list** (the array substitute recommended for implementing your algorithms in Python) is:

```
my_list = [None]*4
```

Python's list container does not have to store a declared number of data items. This means that the syntax for creating an empty list of a given length does not look a lot like the pseudocode array declaration. `[None]*4` creates a list that has four empty data spaces. The Python code above then assigns the list created to the `my_list` identifier. This is equivalent to:

```
my_array[0:3] OF <datatype>
```

in pseudocode. You can see what is happening with the Python code in the interactive session below.

> **KEY WORD**
>
> **list:** a container data type that is available to Python programmers that can be used to implement algorithms requiring arrays.

INTERACTIVE SESSION

```
>>> my_list = [None]*4
>>> print(my_list)
[None, None, None, None]
>>>
```

Further Information:

Python programmers would normally just declare an empty list such as:

```
my_list = []
```

to which data items can be added as required.

10.2 Initialising arrays

At some point, you will want to create an array that is already filled with content. In pseudocode, it is achieved like this:

```
greek_letters ← ['Alpha', 'Beta', 'Gamma', 'Delta', 'Epsilon']
```

This is now a predefined array with five spaces that will only store strings. In Python, the equivalent code would be:

```
greek_letters = ['Alpha', 'Beta', 'Gamma', 'Delta', 'Epsilon']
```

10.3 Using arrays

Arrays offer programmers advantages over simple variables. As we have seen, they allow many data items to be stored under a single identifier. They give the programmer the ability to reference any individual data item by the appropriate **array index** and to use iteration to read, write or search the array by looping through the data items. This makes arrays particularly effective when working with data records.

> **KEY WORD**
>
> **array index:** a number that refers to an item in an array.

Reading and writing data items

To read a data item, you reference it by the array name and the index number. Look at this array:

```
greek_letters ← ['Alpha', 'Beta', 'Gamma', 'Delta', 'Epsilon']
```

In this array, `greek_letters[2]` holds the data item 'Gamma' (remember that the array index starts at 0, so index number 2 is the third item). Therefore we could output 'Gamma' like this:

```
OUTPUT greek_letters[2]
```

The same logic applies when writing values to an array. The following code would write the letter 'C' to the specified index position, replacing the original data item:

```
greek_letters[2] ← 'C'
```

Now our array of Greek letters would read `'Alpha'`, `'Beta'`, `C`, `'Delta'`, `'Epsilon'`.

The syntax in Python for these two operations, using lists, is almost identical to the pseudocode.

DEMO TASK 10.1

Integer array

Declare an array named 'task' that is capable of holding four integers. Write code to allow the user to input an integer to a selected array position. Then add code to allow the user to output the value held in a selected array position.

Solution

Flowchart 10.1 shows the process of inputting one data item into the array called `task` at position `index`. Flowchart 10.2 shows the output process for one data item. There is nothing special to note here. We have just gone through the processes described above to create the flowcharts.

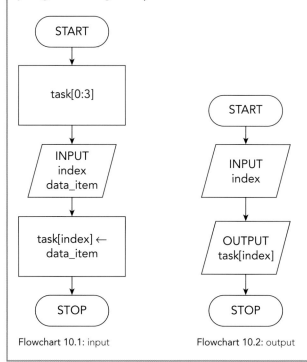

Flowchart 10.1: input   Flowchart 10.2: output

CONTINUED

Here is the pseudocode for the two processes:

```
// Input Pseudocode
task[0:3] OF Integers

INPUT index, data_item
task[index] ← data_item
```
Code snippet 10.1: input

```
// Output Pseudocode
INPUT index
OUTPUT task[index]
```
Code snippet 10.2: output

Note: GUI applications are optional. They are not covered in the syllabuses.

A Python GUI application can be used to produce this system. The interface could be designed as shown in Figure 10.1. A button runs the subroutines for each of the input and output processes. Entry widgets accept the input and display the output. As the functions are so simple, the opportunity has been taken to demonstrate a little more tkinter GUI code.

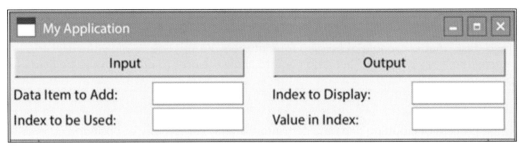

Figure 10.1: A GUI interface design

```
from tkinter import *
# Declare list globally to allow both subroutines access to it
task = [None] * 4

# Functions
def input_data():
    # collect values from Entry boxes
    data_item = int(tbox1.get())
    index = int(tbox2.get())
    # insert new value into array
    task[index] = data_item

def output_data():
    # collect index required
    index = int(tbox3.get())
    # clear output text box and display value
    tbox4.delete(0, END)
    tbox4.insert(END, task[index])
```

CONTINUED

```
#### Build the GUI
# padding is added to some widgets:
# ipadx adds internal padding to left and right
# padx adds external padding to left and right
window = Tk()
window.title('My Application')
bg_colour = 'linen'


# Create two frames
input_frame = Frame(window, bg=bg_colour)
input_frame.grid(row=0, column=0, ipadx=5, ipady=5)
output_frame = Frame(window, bg=bg_colour)
output_frame.grid(row=0, column=1, ipadx=5, ipady=5)


# Create the labels
input_label1 = Label(input_frame, text='Data Item to Add:', bg=bg_colour)
input_label1.grid(row=1, column=0, sticky=W)
input_label2 = Label(input_frame, text='Index to be Used:', bg=bg_colour)
input_label2.grid(row=2, column=0, sticky=W)
output_label1 = Label(output_frame, text='Index to Display:', bg=bg_colour)
output_label1.grid(row=1, column=0, sticky=W)
output_label2 = Label(output_frame, text='Value in Index:', bg=bg_colour)
output_label2.grid(row=2, column=0, sticky=W)


# Create the buttons
inputButton = Button(input_frame, text='Input', command=input_data, width=24)
inputButton.grid(row=0, column=0, columnspan=2, padx=5, pady=5)
outputButton = Button(output_frame, text='Output', command=output_data, width=24)
outputButton.grid(row=0, column=0, columnspan=2, padx=5, pady=5)


# Create the textboxes
tbox1 = Entry(input_frame, width=10)
tbox1.grid(row=1, column=1)
tbox2 = Entry(input_frame, width=10)
tbox2.grid(row=2, column=1)
tbox3 = Entry(output_frame, width=10)
tbox3.grid(row=1, column=1)
tbox4 = Entry(output_frame, width=10)
tbox4.grid(row=2, column=1)


# start tkinter loop
window.mainloop()
```

Code snippet 10.3

PRACTICE TASKS 10.1–10.2

10.1 Integer array program

Write a Python text-based implementation of the algorithm shown in Flowcharts 10.1 and 10.2. Your program will need to have two functions, one for input and one for output. You also need to provide a simple menu system so that the user can choose what to do.

10.2 Externally stored data

Why would it be better to store the array data outside of this program and then initialise the array from this data source at the beginning of the program?

(Note: You will be learning about how to do this in Chapter 13.)

TIP

When testing your code, you may wish to know what is in your array at a particular point in its execution. A simple way to do this is to insert a print statement in your application's code. This will print out the state of your array at that point. Look at this interactive session to see how it works:

INTERACTIVE SESSION

```
>>> letters = ['a', 'b', 'c']
>>> print(letters)
['a', 'b', 'c']
>>>
```

Iteration in arrays

It is possible to use a loop to read all the positions in an array. This allows iterative code to be used to check multiple data values.

Because the size of the array is known, a FOR loop can be used. The counter variable in the FOR loop can be used to iterate through the index positions.

The following pseudocode shows how iteration can be used to output all the data items in a ten-item array:

```
my_array[0:9]
FOR counter 0 TO 9
    OUTPUT my_array[counter]
NEXT
```

Code snippet 10.4

DEMO TASK 10.2

Letters

Declare an array called 'letters' that is capable of holding six single characters. Initialise the array with letters a to f. Write code that allows the user to search the array to identify if any letter input by the user is in the array or not.

Solution

To develop our algorithm, we start with the necessary pseudocode or flowchart structure for initialising an array. Then we build the FOR loop algorithm we learnt about in Chapter 8 shown in Flowchart 10.3.

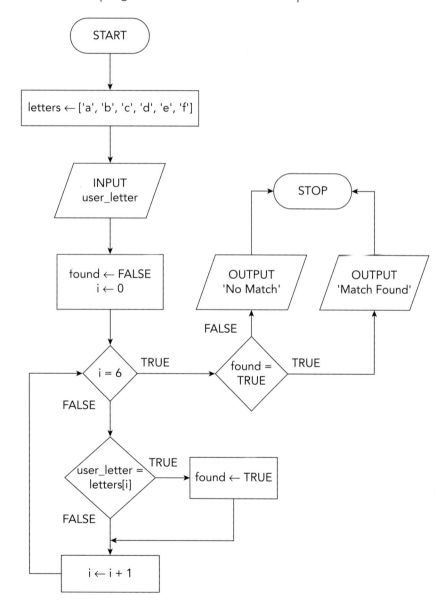

Flowchart 10.3

CONTINUED

Here is the pseudocode design:

```
FUNCTION search
    found ← FALSE
    letters ← ['a', 'b', 'c', 'd', 'e', 'f']
    INPUT user_letter

    FOR i = 0 TO 5
        IF user_letter = letter[i]
          THEN
              found ← TRUE
              ENDFUNCTION
        ENDIF
    NEXT

    IF found ← TRUE
      THEN
        OUTPUT 'Match Found'
      ELSE:
        OUTPUT 'No Match'
    ENDIF
ENDFUNCTION

CALL search
```

Code snippet 10.5

The FOR loop condition follows the indices in the array, from 0 to 5. Once a match has been found, the subroutine is ended. The 'NO Match' message is only shown if the loop has completed.

Below (Code snippet 10.6) is a Python text-based implementation of the letters algorithm. To illustrate how this works, a call to the function has been added after the function definition:

```python
def search():
    # Initialise list to be searched
    letters = ['a','b','c','d','e','f']

    found = False
    user_letter = input('Enter the character to search for: ')
    # Perform search of letters
    for i in range(0,6):
        if user_letter == letters[i]:
            found = True
```

CONTINUED

```
    if found == True:
        print('Match found.')
    else:
        print('No match.')

# Call function
search()
```

Code snippet 10.6

PRACTICE TASKS 10.3–10.6

10.3 Numbers instead of names

Remembering your friends' names can be such a hassle!

a   Design either a flowchart or pseudocode algorithm that starts with an array initialised with six names. The program will ask the user to enter an index number and will then print out the corresponding name.

b   Write a Python implementation of your algorithm.

10.4 Existing names

a   Design either a flowchart or pseudocode algorithm to allow the user to input a search value and then search an array of names held in the array. The program will output either 'Name Found' or 'No Match'.

b   Write a Python implementation of your algorithm. Note that for your program to work, you will need to initialise an array with some names at the start of your program.

10.5 Duplicate names

Design either a flowchart or pseudocode algorithm that will allow a user to input a search value and then search the array to identify if a name held in the array matches. The system will output the index location of any matching name. For example, if the array held the name 'Sameer' in two different index locations, a search for 'Sameer' would output two values.

10.6 Loop more efficiently

Demo Task 10.2 is not very efficient. The loop will search all locations in the array even if a match has been found early in the iteration. For a much larger array, this inefficiency may cause the code to iterate many more times than required.

Rewrite the program using a conditional loop so that the iteration will stop when the match is identified and output 'Match Found'. If the iteration completes without finding a match, your program should output 'No Match'.

Further Information: The Python way

There are many different programming languages. They all have their advantages and disadvantages. One of Python's strengths is the way it works with container variables. You may recall, from Chapter 8, that the reason we use the `range()` function in the FOR loop is because Python FOR loops are of the iterative kind rather than the more traditional counter-controlled FOR loop. Python's FOR loop iterates through sequences or containers – `range()` creates a sequence of numbers. In Demo Task 10.2, the `letters` array was declared and initialised with values. As an array is a kind of container, it can be handled directly by Python's FOR loop. Python's FOR loop is designed to loop through all the items in the container, irrespective of the container's length. This is because lists, unlike arrays, can change length. The normal Python way of looping through `letters` would be like this:

```
# Perform search of letters
for letter in letters:
    if user_letter == letter:
        print('Match found.')
        return
```

Code snippet 10.7

Indeed, Python is so adept at handling containers, there is no need to use a FOR loop at all. Instead, Python programmers would simply use the `in` keyword:

```
# Perform search of letters
if user_letter in letters:
    print('Match found.')
else:
    print('No match.')
```

Code snippet 10.8

Furthermore, as a String in Python is also a container data type, where all characters and spaces are indexed from zero, the following would also function in the same way:

```
# Initialise string to be searched:
letters = 'abcdef'
search = input('Enter the character to search for: ')
# Perform search of letters
if search in letters:
    print('Match found.')
else:
    print('No match.')
```

Code snippet 10.9

Note that this is searching through a String data type and not an array. It is nice to know that all the methods you are learning about arrays are also useful in Python when manipulating String variables.

(continued)

It would be a disservice to the reader, in a book on Python, not to point out its strengths. As a computer science student, however, you are required to iterate through arrays using a counter in a FOR loop. So when implementing your array algorithms, use the format in the solution shown in Demo Task 10.2.

SKILLS FOCUS 10.1

SEARCHING AND SORTING

In computer science there are several **standard methods of solution**. You have used totalling, counting, finding the maximum and minimum, and averaging. Two more standard methods of solution are searching and sorting.

Linear search

A linear search is an algorithm that looks through a group of data one item at a time until the required item is found. We can illustrate how this works with arrays. Here is a pseudocode algorithm for a function that can search through an array of numbers and find the position of the value passed to it:

```
FUNCTION linear_search (array, value)
    FOR i ← 0 TO LENGTH(array)-1
        IF array[i] = value
          THEN
              RETURN i // The position of value in the array
        ENDIF
    NEXT
ENDFUNCTION
```

Code snippet 10.10

and here is the same algorithm in Python with an example array so it will run:

```python
def linear_search(array, value):
    for i in range(len(array)):
        if array[i] == value:
            return i


# Test function:
example = [1, 8, 4, 6, 9, 12]
print(linear_search(example, 9)) # should output 4
```

Code snippet 10.11

Remember an array index starts at 0: 0=1, 1=8, 2=4, etc.

Because searching is such an important process in programming, most computer languages have a built-in function or method to do this. Python is no exception. The following line of code performs a search using the `index()` method:

```python
print(example.index(9)) # should output 4
```

KEY WORD

standard methods of solution: methods of solving problems that occur commonly in computer programs, e.g. linear search, bubble sort, totalling, counting, finding maximum, minimum and average values.

CONTINUED

Bubble sort

This is one of the simplest sorting algorithms. Again, we can use arrays to illustrate how this works. Let's start with an unsorted array called example:

example = [2,6,1,4,3,5]

A bubble sort iterates through the array comparing pairs of values and swapping them if they are in the wrong order. This process is then repeated in another pass until all the values are in order. With the array example the first pass would look like this:

Pass 1:

Compare values 0 and 1: [2,6,1,4,3,5] becomes [2,6,1,4,3,5]

Compare values 1 and 2: [2,6,1,4,3,5] becomes [2,1,6,4,3,5]

Compare values 2 and 3: [2,1,6,4,3,5] becomes [2,1,4,6,3,5]

Compare values 3 and 4: [2,1,4,6,3,5] becomes [2,1,4,3,6,5]

Compare values 4 and 5: [2,1,4,3,6,5] becomes [2,1,4,3,5,6]

The complete pass 2 finishes the job:

[2,1,4,3,5,6] becomes [1,2,3,4,5,6]

The following algorithm passes through the array until one of the passes results in no swaps being made:

```
FUNCTION bubble_sort(array):
    // set a flag to detect when a swap occurs
    changed ← TRUE
    // loop until a pass with no change is detected
    WHILE changed = TRUE DO
        changed ← FALSE
        // loop through each element in the array
        FOR i ← 0 TO LENGTH(array)-1
            // check if the data is in the correct order
            IF array[i] > array[i + 1]
              THEN
                //swap the values
                temp = array[i]
                array[i] = array[i + 1]
                array[i + 1] = temp
            ENDIF
        NEXT
    ENDWHILE
    return array
ENDFUNCTION
```

Code snippet 10.12

CONTINUED

Here is the same algorithm in Python, together with an example array so that the function can be called:

```python
def bubble_sort(array):
    # set a flag to detect when a swap occurs
    changed = True
    # loop until a pass with no change is detected
    while changed == True:
        changed = False
        # loop through each element in the array
        for i in range(len(array)-1):
            # check if the data is in the correct order
            if array[i] > array[i + 1]:
                #swap the items
                temp = array[i]
                array[i] = array[i + 1]
                array[i + 1] = temp
                changed = True
    return array


# Test data
example1 = [2, 6, 1, 4, 3, 5]
example2 = [6, 5, 4, 3, 2, 1]
print(bubble_sort(example1))
print(bubble_sort(example2))
```

Code snippet 10.13

Because sorting is such an important process in programming, most computer languages have a built-in function or method to do this. These are usually a lot more efficient than a bubble sort, often involving an optimised combination of different sorting algorithms. Python is no exception. The following two lines of Python code sorts and prints out example:

```python
example.sort()
print(example)
```

Code snippet 10.14

What is more, this method can also sort an array of strings alphabetically.

Questions

1   In the above illustration of how the bubble sort algorithm works. It stated:
    The complete pass 2:
    [2,6,1,3,4,5] becomes [2,1,4,3,5,6]
    Show how each swap is made in the same way as illustrated in pass 1 above.

2   How many passes would be required to sort [7,2,4,1] in ascending order?

10.4 Groups of arrays

If you need to hold multiple data elements for each data record, it is possible to use arrays in groups. If the items stored in each array are equivalent in some way and the arrays are indexed in the same way, this can prove to be a useful system.

DEMO TASK 10.3

Student exam grades

A program is needed to hold the records shown in Table 10.2.
The programmers decide to store the data in three arrays as shown in Tables 10.3, 10.4 and 10.5.

Student ID	Surname	Computing grade
1001	Khan	A
1002	Luo	C
1003	Agarwal	B
1004	Pontiffe	A

Table 10.2: Student records held for arrays

Index	0	1	2	3
Data item	1001	1002	1003	1004

Table 10.3: Student ID array

Index	0	1	2	3
Data item	Khan	Luo	Agarwal	Pontiffe

Table 10.4: Surname array

Index	0	1	2	3
Data item	A	C	B	A

Table 10.5: Computing grade array

Write the pseudocode to output the Surname and Grade when provided with a given Student ID.

Solution

What we notice, before writing our algorithm, is that all the data for each student is in the same index position in all three arrays. Therefore if we can find the index for the Student ID we can use this ID to access the other information about the student. Here is the algorithm:

CONTINUED

```
INPUT search_ID
FOR i ← 0 TO 2
    IF search_ID = ID[i]
      THEN
         OUTPUT surname[i]
         OUTPUT grade[i]
    ENDIF
NEXT
```

Code snippet 10.15

A Python implementation of this algorithm would look like this:

```
# Initialise arrays so this program works:
ID = ['1001', '1002', '1003', '1004']
surname = ['Khan', 'Luo', 'Agarwal', 'Pontiffe']
grade = ['A', 'C', 'B', 'A']


# Implement the pseudocode algorithm:
search_ID = input('Please enter the student's ID: ')


for i in range(0,3):
    if search_ID == ID[i]:
        print(surname[i])
        print(grade[i])
```

Code snippet 10.16

PRACTICE TASK 10.7

Baby data

a   Design a pseudocode algorithm for a program that could be used to hold and search the following details about children born at a local hospital.

BabyID	Gender	Weight (Kg)	Blood Group
B2003	Male	3.50	O Neg
B2004	Female	3.34	A Pos
B2005	Female	3.62	O Pos

It should be possible to search the system by the BabyID and output all the details of the baby.

b   Write and test a text-based Python implementation of this algorithm.

CHALLENGE TASK 10.1

Advanced baby data

Make a new version of your Python program from Practice Task 10.7 so that it is possible to:

- Search by Gender – outputting the BabyID of all records that match the gender.

- Output the average weight of all the babies in the array.

10.5 Two-dimensional arrays

The arrays used so far in this chapter are sometimes referred to as **one-dimensional arrays**. An alternative to using several arrays is to use a **two-dimensional array**.
The data from Table 10.2 in Demo Task 10.3 could be stored in a single table with two sets of indices (plural for index) as shown in Table 10.6.

Index	0	1	2
0	1001	Khan	A
1	1002	Luo	C
2	1003	Agarwal	B
3	1004	Pontiffe	A

Table 10.6: Student records in a 2D array

Using the two indices in Table 10.6, we can access the data in each cell in a similar way to using coordinates:

```
cell[0][0] is 1001
cell[0][2] is 1003
cell[2][1] is C
```

The pseudocode for declaring the array in Table 10.6 would be:

```
student: ARRAY[0:3][0:2] OF String
```

The pseudocode to output values in this two-dimensional array is:

```
OUTPUT student[0][0]    // outputs '1001'
OUTPUT student[1][2]    // outputs 'Agarwal'
OUTPUT student[1][3]    // outputs 'Pontiffe'
```

KEY WORDS

one-dimensional array: a linear array with a single index set. Contains one row of data with multiple elements; each element is identified by a unique index number.

two-dimensional array: an array with two index sets. Contains multiple rows of data with multiple columns. Each individual element identified by a combination of both row and column index.

TIP

Which index is on the x-axis and which is on the y-axis is unimportant. While we may find it helpful to visualise a two-dimensional array as a grid, the array is not stored as a grid in the computer's memory.

PRACTICE TASK 10.8

Baby data 2

a   Rewrite your algorithm from Practice Task 10.7, but use a two-dimensional array to store the babies' data rather than separate arrays.

b   Write and test a text-based Python implementation of this algorithm.

TIP

The array can be initialised like this:
```
baby_data ← [['B2003', 'Male', '3.5' , 'O Neg'],
             ['B2004', 'Female', '3.34', 'A Pos'],
             ['B2005', 'Female', '3.62', 'O Pos']]
```

CHALLENGE TASK 10.2

Advanced baby data 2

Rewrite your Python program from Practice Task 10.8 using a two-dimensional array.

When to use two-dimensional arrays

In the examples so far, there has not been a good reason to use two-dimensional arrays instead of groups of one-dimensional arrays. However, when there are many records instead of just a few, it becomes easier to manage a two-dimensional array.

There are also benefits to be had when relationships across the two-dimensional arrays are important rather than just a vertical position. For example, a lot of games involve maps divided into 2D grids. In such a situation, the two-dimensional array indices can be thought of as coordinates in the map. If a programmer wanted to represent a chessboard, a two-dimensional array provides several advantages:

- The indices provide a coordinate system to represent the board.

- Finding where pieces can move to can be calculated with simple functions that, for example, add or take away 2 from one index (the green squares) and add or take away 1 from the other (the red squares) for knights (see Figure 10.2 on the following page).

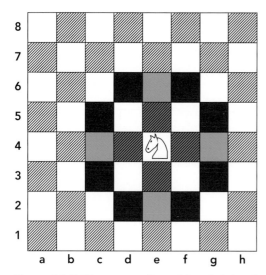

Figure 10.2: The moves allowed for a knight when playing chess

- A loop can be used to check whether a piece is on any square in a row or column, or even a diagonal.

- When we use two-dimensional arrays, all the data in the array can be read or written using two nested loops. For example, in a two-dimensional array that stores the positions of all of the chess pieces. To search for the location of the white queen, 'wQ', the following nested loops can be used:

```python
# Initialise an empty 8 x 8 'array'
# [0][0] is bottom left of board.
chessboard = [[None for i in range(8)] for j in range(8)]


# Add two pieces:
chessboard[0][0] = 'wC' # white Castle
chessboard[3][0] = 'wQ' # white Queen


# Search for white Queen:
for row_counter in range(0,8):
    for col_counter in range(0,8):
        if chessboard[col_counter][row_counter] == 'wQ':
            print('(' + str(col_counter) + ', ' + str(row_counter) + ')')
```

Code snippet 10.17

Further Information: Other container data types

At this point, it is worth pointing out that with Python's rich set of container data types, there are other ways of solving the problem outlined. Indeed, the flexibility of Python's container data types and the libraries of methods that work with them is comprehensive. Lists, for example, can expand and contract; they can contain a mixture of data types, including other containers. Dictionaries provide a kind of unordered list where the programmer chooses the key (instead of being limited to indices of 0, 1, 2, etc.). These keys could

(continued)

be a String or number type variable and can contain a mixture of data types, including other containers. And of course, as discussed earlier, Strings can be treated as container data types in Python. By learning Python, you have a very powerful programming language at your disposal.

Python's other container data types are optional and beyond the scope of the syllabuses and this book. If you are interested in learning more about Python's container data types you might like to try one of the Coding Club level two books, also by Chris Roffey, which explore Python's containers in a less formal way.

10.6 Array reference for implementation in Python

Items can be added using simple index calls:

Declaring an empty array of length 4:

Pseudocode:

```
my_array[0:3] OF <data type>
```

Python code:

```
my_list = [None]*4
print(my_list
Output: [None, None, None, None]
```

Items can be assigned using simple index calls:

Pseudocode:

```
my_array[0] ← 2
my_array[1] ← 4
my_array[2] ← 6
my_array[3] ← 8
```

Python code:

```
my_list[0] = 2
my_list[1] = 4
my_list[2] = 6
my_list[3] = 8
```

Items can be accessed using simple index calls:

Pseudocode:

```
OUTPUT my_array[0]
Output: 2
```

Python code:

```
print(my_list[0])
Output: 2
print(my_list)
Output: [2, 4, 6, 8]
```

Iterate through an array with a For Loop:

Pseudocode:

```
FOR i = 0 TO 3
    OUTPUT my_array[i]
NEXT
Output:
2
4
6
8
```

Python code:

```
for i in range(0,4):
    print(my_list[i])

Output:
2
4
6
8
```

Two-dimensional arrays need to be declared differently in Python (or else you will get unexpected errors). Reading and writing can then proceed in the same way for both pseudocode and Python:

Declaring an empty 2D array of length 3 × 3 in pseudocode:

```
my_array[0:2][0:2] OF <data type>
```

Declaring an empty 2D array of length 4 × 4 in Python:

```
my_2D_list = [[None for i in range(3)] for j in range(3)]
print(my_2D_list)
```

```
Output: [[None, None, None], [None, None, None], [None, None, None]]
```

SUMMARY

An array is a data type that can hold a set of variables of the same data type under a single identifier.
When an array is declared, its size is defined. In Python, indices start from zero.
Each element or data item in an array can be referenced by its index.
The index can be used to read or write values in an array.
A two-dimensional array has two sets of indices that can be thought of as coordinates in a table.
A FOR loop can be used to iterate through the index locations in an array. The loop counter is used to identify successive index numbers.
Holding records that consist of more than one data item can be achieved by the use of multiple arrays. Data for each record is held at the same index position in the different arrays.
When using Python to implement algorithms involving arrays, a list is used as a substitute for an array.

END-OF-CHAPTER TASKS

The number of data items in the following tasks is deliberately small to allow you to code and test your system. In a written examination, you would not normally be expected to create an array. The questions are more likely to test your ability to write algorithms that make use of a provided array.

1   An array, numbers, is used to hold the following integer values:

17	103	36	42	85	3	64	98	55	11

  a   Write a pseudocode algorithm for a program that will use an array called numbers to hold this data. The program will use the array to output the following values:

   i   The sum of the numbers in the array.

   ii   The largest and smallest numbers in the array.

   iii   The mean average of the numbers in the array.

The program must have an option for the user to be able to change individual numbers in the array.

    b Will your algorithm need to be altered if the array holds 1000 numbers?

    c Write a text-based Python implementation of your algorithm.

2 Create a program called `rainbow.py` that begins with the following code:

```
# rainbow.py
from turtle import *


pensize(50)
line_length = 20
colours = ['Red', 'Orange', 'Yellow', 'Blue', 'Green', 'Indigo', 'Violet']
```

    a Write a turtle program that iterates through `colours` and draws pattern **a**, below.

    b Write a turtle program that iterates through `colours` twice and draws pattern **b**, below.

    c Write a turtle program that uses `random.choice(colours)` to pick random colours from `colours` and draws a pattern like **c**, below.

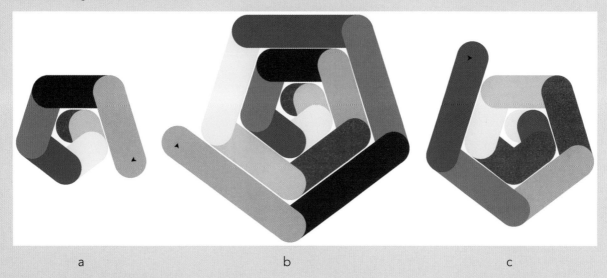

         a   b   c

3 An array is to be used to identify if a six-digit number is a palindrome. A palindrome reads the same both forwards and backwards, for example, 192291, 788887, 123321, 999999, 114411.

    a Write a pseudocode algorithm for a program that asks a user to input each of the 6 digits in turn. Your program should store them in an array indexed from 0. For example, if the number 786678 was entered it would be stored as follows:

Index	0	1	2	3	4	5
Number	7	8	6	6	7	8

    Once the number has been entered, the system will identify if the number is a palindrome and output an appropriate message.

    b Write a Python implementation of your algorithm and run some tests to check that your program works as expected.

CONTINUED

4 Write a pseudocode algorithm for a program that uses a set of one-dimensional arrays to hold the following data about animals for sale:

Type	Colour	Suggested minimum age of children in household	Breed
Cat	White	5	Persian
Dog	Black and white	12	Husky
Dog	Grey	1	Poodle
Parrot	Blue and red	8	Macaw

Your program should allow the user to be able to carry out the following searches:

- Input an animal type; output all the data about animals of that type.

- Input the age of youngest child in the household; output a list of suitable animals.

- Input both the preferred type of animal and the age of youngest child; output the data about suitable animals.

5 Re-do Task 4 using a single two-dimensional array.

> **TIP**
>
> For Tasks 4 and 5, ask the user to input 18 if they have no children. This will mean an age will always be available to compare in the array.

## Chapter 11

Checking inputs

- understand the need for accuracy of inputs

- know how to design validation and verification routines using flowcharts or pseudocode

- understand the role and use of a range of validation and verification techniques:

  - presence check

  - range check

  - length check

  - type check

  - format check

  - check digit

- know how to program validation into your algorithms.

Introduction

Organisations rely on the accuracy of their data when making decisions. Inaccurate data can result in poor decisions, possibly with devastating results. Consider the situation of a doctor receiving inaccurate medical data about a patient, or a firefighter being given inaccurate data about wind speed and direction. The largest source of inaccuracies is during the data entry process. Therefore, it is important that systems are designed to help increase the accuracy of data entry.

11.1 Validation

Validation is the process of programming a system to automatically check that data falls within a set of specified criteria. While validation cannot guarantee that data entered is accurate, it does ensure that it is reasonable. Systems should also filter out obvious mistakes. For example, if a system were recording the height of students, it would be reasonable to expect that they were all under 3 metres tall. Programming the system to reject data entries above 3 metres would help to remove obvious errors. However if a student's height was measured at 1.4 metres, but inaccurately entered as 1.04 metres, the system would still accept the value because it meets the validation criteria.

Table 11.1 shows different types of validation checks:

KEY WORD

validation: the process of programming a system to automatically check that data satisfies a set of specified input criteria; for example, passwords must be longer than six characters.

TIP

Validation does not make data input accurate – this is a common misconception.

Validation type	Description	Example
Presence check	Checks that required data has been input. The system will reject groups of data where required fields have been left blank. This is often used with data-collection forms.	Online order where 'Email Address' must be provided.
Range check	Checks data falls within a reasonable range. Data outside the expected range is rejected. It is possible to have data where the range limit is only applicable to one extreme. For example, the volume of a vessel cannot be zero but may not have an upper limit. This is known as a 'limit check'.	Age must be between 0 and 130 inclusive. Day of the month must be between 1 and 31 inclusive. Percentage score in an exam must be between 0 and 100 inclusive.
Length check	Checks that data entered is of a reasonable length. Data items that have a length outside the expected values are rejected. Normally used with text-based inputs.	Surname must be between 1 and 25, inclusive, characters long. A password must have more than six characters.
Type check	Checks that a data item is of a particular data type. It will reject any input that is of a different type.	Stock items in a shop must be entered as an integer. Age will be numeric (e.g. it will not accept 'over 21').
Format check	Checks that a data item matches a predetermined pattern and that the individual elements of the data item have particular values or data types.	Date of birth will be in the format dd/mm/yyyy. Mobile telephone numbers will be in the format NNNNN NNNNNN where N is a digit.

(continued)

Validation type	Description	Example
Check digit	Checks that a numerical data item has been entered accurately. Extra digit(s) are added to the number based on a calculation that can be repeated, enabling the number to be checked by repeating the calculation and comparing the calculated check digit with the value entered.	A barcode includes a check digit. ISBNs (book numbers) include a check digit.

Table 11.1: Validation checks

11.2 Verification

Verification confirms the integrity of data as it is input into the system or when it is transferred between different parts of a system. Data integrity refers to the correctness of data during and after processing. Although the format of the data may be changed by processing, if data integrity has been maintained the data will remain a true and accurate representation of the original. Copying data should clearly not change the data values.

Most verification techniques are undertaken by the person inputting the data. Visual checks can involve providing a summary of the data just entered, by the person inputting the data, to be checked. This summary has to be confirmed as correct or re-edited. Another form of verification that you could program is double entry verification. In this case the data item is entered twice and the system compares the input values and produces an error message if there is a difference between the two entries. You may have come across this on a web-form where you have been asked to type your email address or password twice.

11.3 Programming validation into your systems

Running code without passing the correct values to the variables will cause a program to crash or provide unexpected results. Run any of your programs without inputting the required numeric values and you will receive an error message. This is illustrated in the following interactive session:

INTERACTIVE SESSION

```
>>> a = '1'
>>> b = 2
>>> c = a + b
Traceback (most recent call last):
    File "<pyshell#2>", line 1, in <module>
        c = a + b
TypeError: can only concatenate str (not "int") to str
>>>
```

KEY WORDS

verification: a process that confirms the integrity of data as it is input into the system or when it is transferred between different parts of a system, for example a CAPTCHA image used to prove data is being entered by a human.

data integrity: the correctness of data during and after processing.

visual check: a verification technique where previously entered data is presented back to either the data entry person, or someone else, to check and confirm it is correct.

double entry: a verification technique where the same data has to be entered twice and the computer checks that both entries are the same before accepting the data as valid.

This is important when getting user input of numbers in Python as the `input()` function always returns String data types. Python will not cast a String to a number without being explicitly asked to. Should this happen in a published program, the system would crash unexpectedly.

To avoid this type of error, validation should first try to cast the user input to a number with either `int()` or `float()`. If this process fails, the data entered should be rejected because a number of the correct sort was not entered.

Presence check validation

DEMO TASK 11.1

Supply your name

Code is required to check whether a user has input a value into a required field (firstname) in an online form. If the data is present, it will pass the check. Note there is no guarantee that the name supplied will be in the correct format so additional validation may be required.

Solution

Our algorithm for this task needs to start with inputting the user's first name. The validation process can then take place in a loop. The idea is that, while the data input is incorrect, the algorithm needs to keep giving the user another chance to enter the data correctly. When the test is passed, the program can continue. In this case, the test is simply whether there is any data. The algorithm can be seen in the flowchart in Flowchart 11.1.

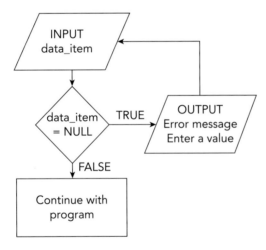

Flowchart 11.1

CONTINUED

In text-based programs, a WHILE loop can be used to check the presence of the input. If the data is missing, then the user can be prompted again to enter the required data.

```python
data_item = input('Insert text value: ')

while data_item == '':
    data_item = input('Please input text value: ')

# program continues
```

Code snippet 11.1

Further Information:

In GUI applications, the execution of code is triggered by an event such as a button press. The trigger cannot be controlled from within a WHILE loop in the same way. A different approach is therefore needed.

For comparison with the text-based code in Code snippet 11.1, the following code provides a GUI implementation. A message is displayed in a label widget that previously held an empty String and so was not visible:

```python
def button_click():
    if text_box.get() == '':
        my_label.config(text='Enter text here: ')
    else:
        # program continues with for example:
        user_input = text_box.get()
```

Code snippet 11.2

Note how this does not use a WHILE loop because the text box entry only has to be processed if the button is pressed. The tkinter `mainloop()` method, however, is running in its own loop that constantly checks for all events, including button presses.

PRACTICE TASK 11.1

Last name

a   Produce a flowchart and the pseudocode for a system that will ask for a last name and provide an error message if it is not present.

b   Write a Python implementation of your algorithm.

CHALLENGE TASK 11.1

First name

a   Produce the flowchart and pseudocode for a system that asks a user to input their first name and checks that it does not include any numbers in it and only includes upper case and lower case unaccented letters. For example, *freddy* is accepted but *Fr3ddy* and Sébastien are not.

b   Write a Python implementation of your algorithm.

TIPS

For Challenge Task 11.1a, you may find it useful to put the characters in the name into an array by casting the string with the `ARRAY(<string>)` function.

For Challenge Task 11.1b, remember that an 'array' of characters from a string can be created with Python's `list()` function.

Range check validation

DEMO TASK 11.2

Day of the month

A system is required that asks the user to input the day of the month. The system should only accept numbers from 1 to 31 and reject all others.

Solution

The principle for this algorithm is the same as for the last validation technique. Our algorithm needs to keep offering another chance for the user to enter their input while it does not pass our test. In this case it is a simple check to see if the data is less than 1 or more than 31. If it is then the algorithm needs to loop back. When the data is in range the program can continue. This is illustrated below (Code snippet 11.3), in pseudocode this time. Note again the use of a WHILE loop.

```
INPUT day

WHILE day < 1 OR day > 31 DO
    OUTPUT Error message
    INPUT day
ENDWHILE


// Continue with program
```

Code snippet 11.3

The algorithm in Code snippet 11.3 can be programmed in Python like this:

```
day = int(input('Enter the day of the month: '))

while day < 1 or day > 31:
    day = int(input('Enter a value between 1 and 31: '))

# Program continues
```

Code snippet 11.4

PRACTICE TASK 11.2

What month?

a   Produce a flowchart and the pseudocode for a system that will ask for the month and provide an error message if it is not 1 to 12 inclusive.

b   Write a Python implementation of your algorithm.

CHALLENGE TASK 11.2

Day of the week

a   Produce a flowchart and the pseudocode for a system that will ask for the day of the week and provide an error message if it does not match one of: Monday, Tuesday, Wednesday, Thursday, Friday, Saturday or Sunday.

b   Write a Python implementation of your algorithm.

Length check validation

DEMO TASK 11.3

Long passwords

A system is required that asks the user to input a password of six or more characters. The system should only accept passwords with six or more characters and produce an error message if the submitted password contains five or fewer.

Solution

Our code needs to calculate the length of the password. It then follows a similar process to a range check using a WHILE loop to check the input against the required criteria. If the data input is acceptable, the system should continue to run; if not, the system will output an error message to the user. The algorithm is shown in Flowchart 11.2:

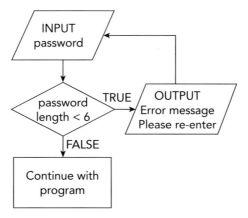

Flowchart 11.2

CONTINUED

The algorithm in Flowchart 11.2 can be programmed in Python like this:

```
password = input('Enter password: ')
while len(password) < 6:
    password = input('Your password must have six or more characters: ')


# Program continues
```

Code snippet 11.5

PRACTICE TASK 11.3

Password length

Write a pseudocode version of the algorithm provided in Demo Task 11.3.

CHALLENGE TASK 11.3

Complex password

a   Produce a flowchart and the pseudocode for a system that will ask for a password of six or more characters and includes both a letter and a number.

b   Write a Python implementation of your algorithm.

SKILLS FOCUS 11.1

Although programmers are often asked to build systems that ask for passwords like the one in Challenge Task 11.3, it is currently recommended that passwords take the form of three or four unrelated words. Therefore, if you are asked to produce a program with a password field this should make your task slightly easier!

Questions

1   What two kinds of validation are required for such a password?

2   Which of the following are currently thought to be good passwords?

- onceuponatime

- G30graPHY

- lemonvansgreetflu

- theclockswerestrikingthirteen

Type check validation

DEMO TASK 11.4

Day of the month 2

A system is required that asks the user to input the day of the month. The system should only accept integers as input.

Solution

Our code will need to identify the data type. It will then use a WHILE loop to check the input against the required criteria. If the data input is acceptable, the system will continue to run; if not, the system will output an error message to the user.

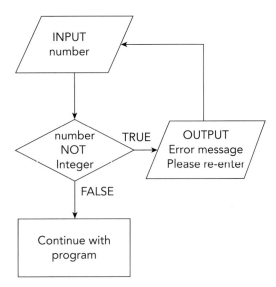

Flowchart 11.3

While the flowchart solution (Flowchart 11.3) for type check validation is reasonably straightforward, the code approach is more complex. Python's `input()` function returns a String, so we would normally cast this to an Integer with the `int()` function. However, if the input is not an Integer then the program will crash. What we want to do is evaluate the form of the input String. There is a function called `eval()` that we can use that does just this and then returns the appropriate type. Look at how this works in this interactive session:

INTERACTIVE SESSION

```
>>> number = input('Enter number: ')
Enter number: 2.1
>>> type(number)
<class 'str'>
>>> number = eval(number)
>>> type(number)
<class 'float'>
>>>
```

CONTINUED

So one coded solution would be:

```
number = input('Please input a number: ')
while type(eval(number)) is not int:
    number = input('Not an integer. Please enter an integer: ')
# Program continues
```

Code snippet 11.6

A more advanced approach is to have a go at casting to an Integer and then use Python's built-in `try...except` error handling code like this:

```
number = input('Please input a number: ')
while True:
    try:
        int(number)
        break
    except:
        number = input('Not an integer. Please enter an integer: ')
# Program continues
```

Code snippet 11.7

Notice how this solution puts the exception handling code in an infinite loop and then uses the `break` keyword to exit when the required conditions are met.

PRACTICE TASK 11.4

Number month

a   Produce a flowchart and the pseudocode for a system that will ask for the month and provide an error message if a non-integer is provided.

b   Write a Python implementation of your algorithm.

CHALLENGE TASK 11.4

Days of the month

a   Produce a flowchart and the pseudocode for a system that will ask for the day of the month and provide an appropriate error message if the input is a non-integer, less than 1 or more than 31.

b   Write a Python implementation of your algorithm.

Format check validation

DEMO TASK 11.5

Date format

A form is required that asks the user to input the date in the format dd/mm/yyyy. The system will be required to check each element of the user input to check it matches the required pattern.

Solution

Our code will be required to check each element of the user input to ensure it matches a predetermined pattern. If the date matches the pattern, the system will continue to run; if not, the system will output an error message to the user.

```
INPUT date

WHILE date IS NOT in format dd/mm/yyyy DO
    OUTPUT Error message
    INPUT date
ENDWHILE

// Continue with program
```
Code snippet 11.8

As you might expect, Python has built-in libraries for validating a number of data types. As we are trying to ensure the integrity of this data, it is best, whenever possible, to use tried and tested methods. As this might well be a common requirement in a program, it might be best to implement the validation in a function and then call it. The code below (Code snippet 11.9) imports the `datetime` methods from the `datetime` library and then implements the algorithm in the `validate_date()` function. A call for user input and the use of the function have been added to show how to use this function whenever a user is required to input a date.

```python
from datetime import datetime

def validate_date(d):
    while True:
        try:
            return datetime.strptime(d, '%d/%m/%Y')
        except:
            d = input('Date must be in the format dd/mm/yyyy: ')

date = input('Please enter a date: ')
date = validate_date(date)

# Program continues
```
Code snippet 11.9

CONTINUED

The validate_date() function tries to return a Python date data type that is now much safer and more flexible for the programmer to use than the initial String. If the strptime() function does not get passed a String in the pattern specified, an exception is thrown and the user is asked to try again. The return keyword is the equivalent of a break command but also returns a value. There are many patterns that can be asked for: '%d/%m/%Y' matches the requested format. More information about the strptime() function is available on the official Python documentation website.

The try ... except code structure works a bit like if ... else. The program attempts to run the code in the try block but if it fails and would cause an error, instead of the program crashing, the code in the except block is run.

PRACTICE TASK 11.5

Date format

a Produce a flowchart and the pseudocode for a system that will ask for the date and provide an error message if it does not match the format yyyy/mm/dd.

b Write a Python implementation of your algorithm.

CHALLENGE TASK 11.5

Letters, hyphens and apostrophes

a Produce a flowchart and the pseudocode for a system that will ask for the user's firstname and provides an error message if it does not start with a capital letter. The algorithm should check that the name also only contains letters, hyphens and apostrophes.

b Write a Python implementation of your algorithm.

Check digit validation

DEMO TASK 11.6

ISBN check digits

A system is required that implements ISBN-13 check digit validation. Produce a flowchart for this system. Write a Python implementation of your algorithm.

Solution

Flowchart 11.4 shows an algorithm for an ISBN-13 check digit validation. In ISBN-13 validation, the 13th digit is removed as this is the check digit. All the other numbers are assigned a 1 or 3, alternating from 1. These numbers are used as multipliers for their corresponding digits. All the products are added together, the remainder after dividing this by 10 is found. The remainder is then subtracted from 10. This should match the check digit if the ISBN number is correct.

CONTINUED

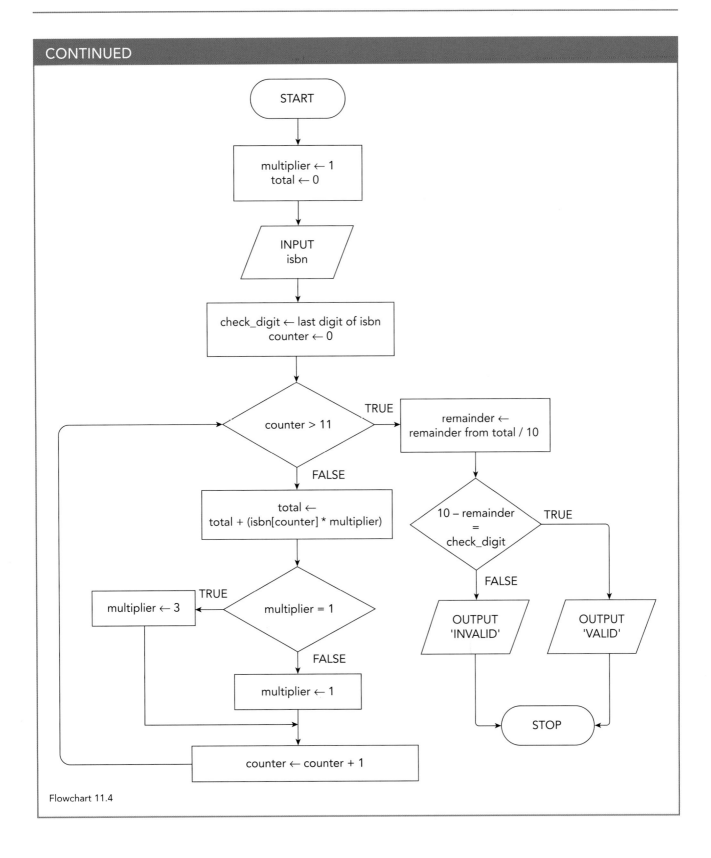

Flowchart 11.4

CONTINUED

The ISBN number, taken as input, is a pseudo number. This is input as a string and each digit is accessed by the string index (starting from zero). If you need a reminder on how indexing works, it was introduced in Chapter 10.

```
multiplier = 1
total = 0
# Input an ISBN-13 number as a string
isbn = input('Input an ISBN-13 number with no spaces: ')
# Obtain the 13th digit (all characters in string are numbered from zero)
check_digit = int(isbn[12])


# Iterate through the first 12 digits of the ISBN number
for i in range(12):
    total = total + (int(isbn[i]) * multiplier)
    if multiplier == 1:
        multiplier = 3
    else:
        multiplier = 1
remainder = total % 10


if (10 - remainder) == check_digit:
    print('ISBN valid')
else:
    print('Invalid ISBN number')
```

Code snippet 11.10

PRACTICE TASK 11.6

ISBN numbers

Write a pseudocode implementation of the algorithm provided in Demo Task 11.6.

CHALLENGE TASK 11.6

Barcodes

An EAN-8 barcode (used on small packages) consists of an eight-digit number where the first seven digits provide a code and the last digit is a check digit. The check digit is calculated, from the previous seven digits, in the following way:

- Add the digits in the odd-numbered positions (first, third, fifth, seventh.) together and then multiply the answer by three.

- Add the digits in the even-numbered positions (those in positions two four, and six) being careful not to include the check digit).

CONTINUED

- Add the results of the two above calculations together and then find the remainder of the result when divided by 10. This is the check digit.

a   Produce a flowchart and the pseudocode for a system that inputs the 12 digits from a barcode and outputs 'valid' or 'invalid' using the system just described. Assume the digits have already been added to an array such as:

```
barcode ← [3, 4, 7, 8, 6, 6, 2, 2]
```

b   Write a Python implementation of your algorithm.

SUMMARY

Accuracy of data entry is an important consideration in system design. Inaccurate data can lead to inaccurate outputs.
Validation is a technique in which the system checks data input against a set of predetermined rules.
Validation can identify obvious errors by detecting data that fails to meet the validation rules.
Validation is able to ensure that data input is reasonable but cannot guarantee data accuracy.
Six main forms of validation are used to check data as it is input: • Presence checks ensure that data has been input. • Range checks ensure that data falls within a predetermined range of values. • Length checks ensure that data inputs contain a predetermined number of characters. • Type checks ensure that data input is of a certain data type. • Format checks ensure that data input meets a predetermined format, such as dd/mm/yyyy. • Check digits are calculated from numerical data, such as a barcode, and added to the end of the data.
Verification checks the integrity of data when it is entered into the system. This is often completed by the person inputting the data.
Two common methods of verification are: • Checking the input data against the original document or record. • Double entry in which the data is entered twice and the entries compared to identify differences.

END-OF-CHAPTER TASKS

1 Program a function that will validate a username and password from the user. All inputs must be validated against the following criteria:

- The username must consist of only lower case letters and hyphens.

- The password must start with an upper case P and then consist of six integers. e.g. P537917

The function will be passed the parameters of the username and password and will return a Boolean value to indicate if the inputs match the validation criteria.

2 a Produce a flowchart or pseudocode for a system that makes use of the function in End-of-Chapter Task 1. If the validation is completed successfully, the system will output 'Welcome'. If the validation check is failed once, the system will output 'Error. Please try again'. If the validation check fails twice, the system will output 'Locked Out' and exit the program.

Note: GUI applications are optional. They are not covered in the syllabuses.

b Produce either a text-based or GUI implementation of your algorithm.

TIP

For Task 2, there are two ways of exiting a program in Python before reaching the end. First, you can wrap your main program in its own function such as `main()` and then call it at the end of your script – when you want to exit `main()` you use the keyword `return`. The second method is to import the `sys` module and then call `sys.exit()`.

## Chapter 12

Testing

IN THIS CHAPTER YOU WILL:

- learn about the importance of testing systems
- identify logical, syntax and runtime errors
- learn how to dry run algorithms using trace tables
- identify appropriate valid, invalid and boundary data when testing systems.

Introduction

In common with many products, it is important to make sure systems work as expected before they are released to the final user. The complexity and critical nature of the system will determine how much testing is to be completed. For example, the computerised air traffic control system at an airport is more critical than a smartphone game and, therefore, will have undergone far more extensive testing as failure could be catastrophic.

There are several notable examples of disasters caused by poor testing. The destruction of the unmanned *Ariane 5* space rocket, due to the failure of untested code, is one of the most costly examples ever. The financial losses were measured in billions of dollars. An article published in *The New York Times* magazine in December 1996 has information about the software error that caused the disaster. You will be able to find the article if you search online for 'Ariane disaster'.

12.1 When to test

Testing can be broken into two distinct areas: alpha testing and beta testing.

Alpha testing

Alpha testing is completed during the programming of a system. It checks that each part of a program works as expected before being combined to make a complete system. Testing during the programming stage can also help trace the source of unexpected outcomes.

Beta testing

Beta testing is formal testing that takes place once the system has been completed to ensure that the whole system meets expectations. The product that has been developed is installed on the systems where it is intended to be used. Alternatively, it will be normal users of the new system who are testing it just by using it.

12.2 Debugging

Debugging is the process of detecting faults that cause errors in a program. This can be achieved by observing error messages produced by the IDE or by investigating unexpected results. The types of error that can occur are divided into three groups: logical errors, syntax errors and runtime errors.

Logical errors

Logical errors are errors in the design of the program that allow it to run but produce unexpected results. They can result from the use of an incorrect formula or the incorrect use of control structures such as IF statements or loops. Examples include IF statements with incorrect conditions, or loops that iterate the wrong number of times.

KEY WORDS

alpha testing: early testing that takes place when a system has had all of its main features added for the first time.

beta testing: formal testing by users once the system has been completed and passed through a company's internal testing regime.

debugging: a general term for systematically searching for problems in programs that are not working properly and fixing them.

logical errors: result in code that runs but produces unexpected results.

Logical errors are also caused by implementing an incorrect sequence of statements, such as performing a calculation before assigning values to the variables.

Logical errors usually do not produce error messages. The problem is with the logic of the code not the execution of the code.

Syntax errors

Syntax errors are errors in the use of the programming language, such as incorrect punctuation or misspelt variables and control words. Examples include IF statements with missing colons or the incorrect use of assignment. The IDE will usually generate error messages indicating the reason for the error.

Runtime errors

Runtime errors are errors that are only identified during the execution of the program. They can result from mismatched data types, overflow or divide-by-zero operations.

Data type errors include:

- passing String data to an Integer variable, which will probably cause the system to crash
- passing Real data to an Integer variable; the variable will round the input data to the nearest whole number – the system will execute the code but produce unexpected results.

Overflow errors occur when the data passed to a variable is too large to be held by the data type selected. In the theory element of the syllabuses, you will have used this term to describe a situation where a nine-bit binary number is stored in an eight-bit byte. This can often result from calculations during the execution of a program. For example, in some programming languages, the data type Short can be used to hold numbers between -32767 and $+32767$. If a variable of this data type were assigned the result of the square of any number greater than 182, it would produce an overflow error. As Python is a loosely typed language, it works behind the scenes to try and avoid many of these number-type problems.

In mathematics, it is not possible to divide by zero because any number can be divided by zero an infinite number of times. If a program includes a division calculation that divides by a variable holding the value zero, the system will produce a divide-by-zero error. Try dividing a number by zero in your IDE, as shown in the following interactive session:

INTERACTIVE SESSION

```
>>> 3/0
Traceback (most recent call last):
    File "<pyshell#2>", line 1, in <module>
        3/0
ZeroDivisionError: division by zero
>>>
```

KEY WORDS

syntax errors: mistakes made in the code equivalent to spelling and punctuation mistakes in English.

runtime errors: problems with the code that only become evident when the program is run, for example attempting to divide by zero.

overflow errors: overflow errors occur when the data passed to a variable is too large to be held by the data type selected. (Another example of runtime errors.)

divide-by-zero errors: divide-by-zero errors occur when a number is being divided by a variable that has the value zero. A divide-by-zero error will stop the program running. (Another example of runtime errors.)

12.3 IDE debugging tools and diagnostics

KEY WORD

diagnostics: the systematic process of trying to diagnose what is wrong with a program.

Many IDEs include sophisticated **diagnostics** that help identify possible bugs and provide the user with useful error messages. These tools are only able to identify errors in the code, not in the logic of the code, and as a result are unable to identify logical errors. IDLE and Wing IDE 101 provide debugging support for both syntax and runtime errors.

Syntax diagnostics

Syntax errors can be spotted by noticing that the colour of your code in your IDE is not appropriate. For example, if you forget to close the quotation marks at the end of a String, the code will remain green in IDLE until the end of the line. IDLE has a helpful *Check Module* command in the *Run* menu that will find the first instance of an error, highlight it in red and give you an indication of what the problem is, as shown in Figure 12.1.

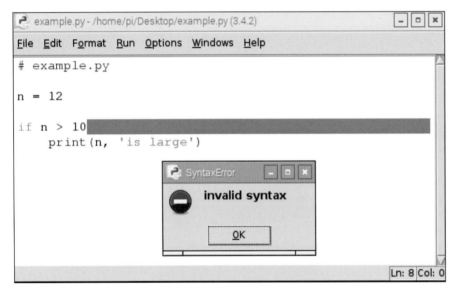

Figure 12.1: Error message in IDLE

```
1   # example.py
2
3   n = 12
4
5   if n > 10
6       print(n, 'is large')
```
Error: Unexpected indentation increase

Figure 12.2: Error message detail in Wing IDE 101

In this instance, the colon is missing from the end of the line. In Wing IDE 101, this kind of error is shown underlined with a zig-zag line, similar to the spell-checker feature in a word processor. Rolling the cursor over the error provides further information, as shown in Figure 12.2.

Runtime diagnostics

Runtime errors are detected during execution of a program and specific error messages are provided. In Figure 12.3, the input() function returns a String variable, but the programmer has tried to use the input in a calculation. The IDE cannot detect that error – it would only occur at runtime (see Figure 12.3).

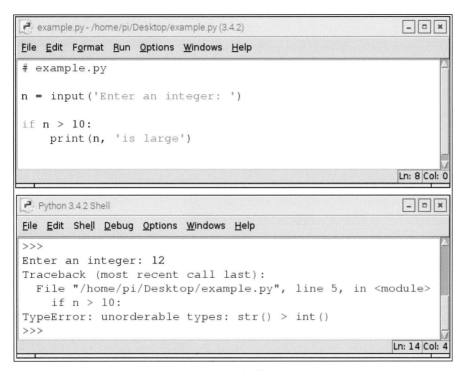

Figure 12.3: IDLE runtime error showing in shell window

PRACTICE TASK 12.1

In the following three scenarios, identify which is the *logical error*, which is *the syntax error* and which is the *runtime error*?

a   A programmer has completed the first subsystem of a new social media app; however, it fails to compile. The IDE highlights a line of the code stating that there is an unexpected end of line.

b   During beta testing, one of the testers reported that the new music creation application he was testing crashed with the following error message: ZeroDivisionError: division by zero.

c   Another beta tester of the same music creation application reported that when she selected piano, the application kept sounding like a harpsichord.

12.4 Identifying logical errors

While the IDE is able to support programmers with syntax and runtime errors, it cannot identify logical errors. The system will operate and process data by following the code that has been written – the IDE is unable to determine if the code contains logical errors that result in unexpected outputs.

The process of identifying logical errors has to be part of the testing process. When unexpected outputs are recognised, it is likely that a logical error will be present in the code. The actual error will also have to be identified manually.

12.5 Dry running

Dry running is the process of working through a section of code manually to locate logical or runtime errors. This type of testing often uses a trace table to record values within a system during its operation. The values traced could relate to the inputs, outputs or variables used in the process. It is usual to use a table with the variables listed as columns and their changing values recorded in rows. An example is shown in the Demo Task 12.1.

KEY WORD
trace tables: a way to test and find bugs in programs. A table is constructed to keep track of the values held in variables as a program is stepped through line by line.

Tracing pseudocode

DEMO TASK 12.1

Trace table

The following pseudocode algorithm is intended to calculate the integer division of x by y.

```
w ← 0
INPUT x
INPUT y


WHILE x > y DO
    x ← x - y
    w ← w +1
ENDWHILE


OUTPUT w
```

Code snippet 12.1

Draw a trace table showing the values held in x, y and w, and any output produced. Start with the initial inputs x = 50 and y = 15.

Solution

The trace table required for this Demo Task is shown in Table 12.1. Comments have been added to help explain the trace table. Comments are not normally required in a formal trace table.

CONTINUED

x	y	w	Output	Comments
		0		Initialisation value.
50	15	0		The new values are input.
35	15	1		x is reduced by 15, w is incremented by 1. ENDWHILE returns to the WHILE condition check. As x > y, the loop continues to run.
20	15	2		x is reduced by 15, w is incremented by 1. ENDWHILE returns to the WHILE condition check. As x > y, the loop continues to run.
5	15	3		x is reduced by 15, w is incremented by 1. ENDWHILE returns to the WHILE condition check. As x < y, the loop exits.
			3	The value in w is output.

Table 12.1: Trace table for algorithm x/y

PRACTICE TASK 12.2

Trace table

The pseudocode algorithm in Demo Task 12.1 contains a logical error. Complete a trace table with the input values of x = 60 and y = 15 to identify the error.

CHALLENGE TASK 12.1

Divider

The following algorithm is designed to find out how many times y divides into x. Create a trace table showing the values of x, y and the output, during the execution of the algorithm, for the following input values:

a   x = 15 and y = 5.

b   x = 18 and y = 4.

```
counter ← -1

INPUT x
INPUT y

WHILE x > -1 DO
    x ← x - y
    counter ← counter + 1
ENDWHILE
OUTPUT counter
```

Tracing a flowchart

Flowchart trace table

Study the flowchart in Flowchart 12.1 and then complete a trace table where the input value is a = 2.

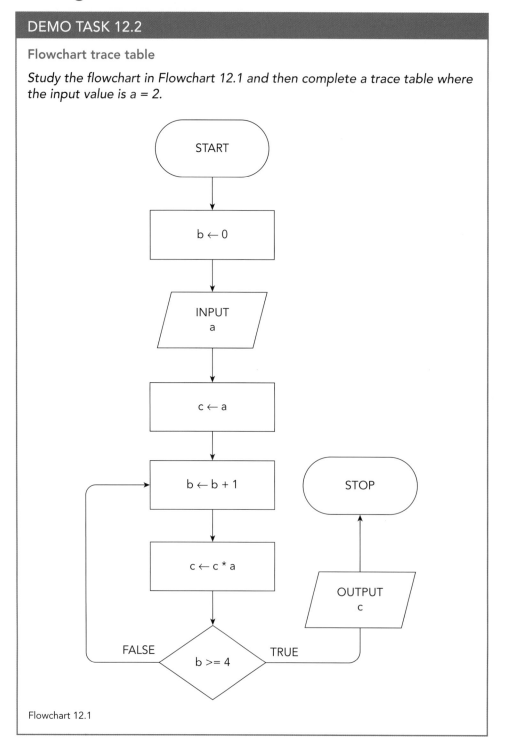

Flowchart 12.1

CONTINUED

Solution

The algorithm for this task is shown in Flowchart 12.1. Follow the flowchart round and see if you can see how the trace table, shown in Table 12.2, was filled in.

a	b	c	Output	Comments
		0		Initialisation value.
2	0	0		Input a.
2	1	2		c ← a b ← b + 1 Will loop as b < 4.
2	1	4		c ← c * a Will loop as b < 4.
2	2	8		b ← b + 1 c ← c * a Will loop as b < 4.
2	3	16		b ← b + 1 c ← c * a Will loop as b < 4.
2	4	32		b ← b + 1 c ← c * a Loop exited as b = 4.
2	4	32	32	Output value in c.

Table 12.2: Trace table for demo task

PRACTICE TASK 12.3

Discussion question

a   What is the aim of the flowchart in Demo Task 12.2?

b   What kind of loop is being suggested here?

CHALLENGE TASK 12.2

Strange output

Study the flowchart in Flowchart 12.2.

Create a trace table showing the values of the variables x, y, w and the output, during the execution of the algorithm, for the following values:

a   x = 17 and y = 6.

b   x = 18 and y = 6.

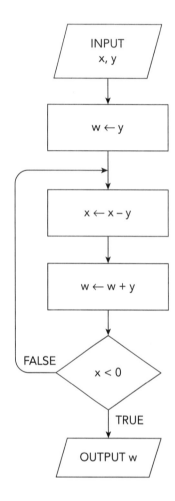

Flowchart 12.2

12.6 Breakpoints, variable tracing and stepping through code

Although IDEs cannot identify logical errors, they do provide tools that assist programmers with this manual process. IDLE and Wing IDE 101, in common with many IDEs, provide the programmer with the ability to run the program one line at a time, displaying the values held in the variables at each step. The programmer is helped to check particular sections of their code by being able to run the program, as normal, until it meets a 'breakpoint'. These are created by the programmer, and will cause the system to run a line of code at a time.

In Wing IDE 101 this process is controlled by the buttons shown in Table 12.3:

Button	Action
🐞	Start or continue debugging until the next breakpoint is reached.
⬇	Start debugging at the first line (or step into the current execution point).
→	Execute the current line of code and then wait.
↱	Step out of the current function or method (useful if there is a long iteration present).

Table 12.3: Debugging actions in Wing IDE 101

The following algorithm has been designed to calculate the number of tins of paint required to cover a wall. The user inputs the length and height of the wall in metres and also the area that can be covered by one tin of paint. The algorithm does not produce the expected result.

```
length = int(input('Enter the length in metres: '))
height = int(input('Enter the height in metres: '))
coverage = int(input('How many square metres are covered by 1 tin? '))

area = length * height
tins = int(area / coverage)
```

Code snippet 12.2

The programmer decides to use the breakpoint diagnostic tool to help identify the error. The breakpoint is inserted after the input sequence as the programmer is happy that the correct inputs are being obtained. To test the system the programmer decides to use a length of 5 metres, a height of 2 metres and a coverage of 8 square metres per tin of paint; the expected area is 10 square metres.

To insert the breakpoint in Wing IDE 101, all that is required is to click with the cursor, next to the desired line number, in this case line 5. When the bug (🐞) is clicked, the code is executed in the normal fashion until the breakpoint is reached. The values of the various variables are viewable in the *Stack Data* panel. If a variable contains a value, hovering over the variable name will also show the value it currently contains.

To execute to line 5 and pause, the *step into current execution point* button ( ) is clicked. This results in the screen shown in Figure 12.4.

Figure 12.4: Wing IDE showing breakpoint variable values

The breakpoint is indicated by the red circle in line 5 and the next line to be executed is highlighted in pink. To delete a breakpoint, click on it again.

In Figure 12.4, it can be seen that the area is 7, not the expected 10. This leads the programmer to realise the error is in the calculation of area. They have incorrectly used addition (5 + 2 = 7) rather than multiplication (5 * 2 = 10).

In IDLE, similar functionality can be achieved by following these steps:

- After writing your script and saving it somewhere, return to the Python shell. The *Debug* menu is only available when the shell window has focus (click on the shell window to bring it to the front).

- From the *Debug* menu select *Debugger*.

- Return to the script file window and either *right-click* or *ctrl-click* on the line of code beginning with area = to create a breakpoint, which will be shown by the line being highlighted.

- From the *Run* menu, choose *Run Module* or press *F5*, which will start executing the program with the *Debugger* on.

- Click the *Go* button in the *Debugger Control* window. The buttons in the *Debug Control* window function in a similar way to the buttons in Wing IDE 101. To keep track of the values in your variables, it is necessary to at least have the Locals and Globals checkboxes selected. See Figure 12.5 on the following page to see what the process looks like in IDLE running on a Raspberry Pi.

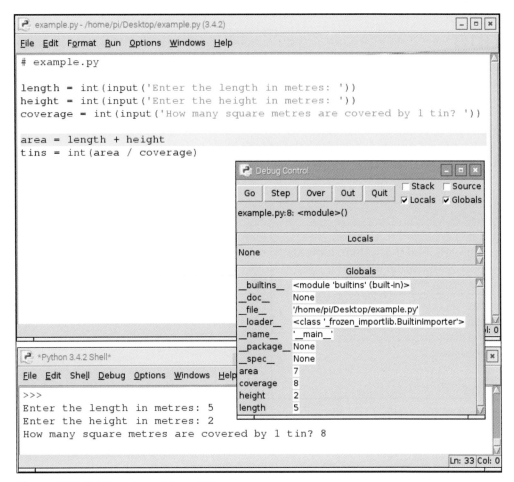

Figure 12.5: IDLE running with the Debugger on

PRACTICE TASK 12.4

Breakpoint

Once this error was fixed, the programmer continued to receive unexpected outputs for some test values.

a   Copy the code (Code snippet 12.2, earlier in the chapter) into a script in your IDE and, using breakpoints and a range of data, identify the remaining error.

b   How should this error be fixed?

TIP

Although it can be tempting to use the IDEs debugger instead of writing out a trace table, sometimes doing this task on paper can show up a tricky bug more easily. Some particularly tricky bugs can only be found by writing out a trace table and then comparing the values you have calculated on paper with the values in the debugger as you step through a program.

12.7 Beta testing

A formal test schedule is designed to test all possible events that a system could experience. It will test normal expected operation as well as extreme inputs or usage. The test schedule will identify the elements of the system to be tested and the data to be used in the tests. Each set of test data and the expected outcome is known as a 'test case'. The data used will fall into three categories, as described in Table 12.4. The example data in Table 12.4 is based on a system designed to calculate the grade achieved by students in an examination. The inputs are the students' marks and the maximum possible mark.

Type of test	Description	Example data
Valid data	Data that is expected to be met in the normal operation of the system. It meets the expected validation rules. The system should produce the expected outcome.	Integer values between zero and the maximum possible score.
Invalid data	Data that will not form part of the expected input range. The system should reject the data and output appropriate error messages.	Non-integer values (it is not possible to get half a mark). Values less than zero or more than the maximum score. Textual inputs, such as 'TEN'.
Boundary data	Data that is at the boundary of the criteria that determine the path of execution of code.	Data that falls at grade boundaries. The grade boundary for an A is 80% and the maximum mark is 100. Data one mark below the grade boundary: 79. Data one mark above the grade boundary: 81.

Table 12.4: Data tested in beta testing

PRACTICE TASK 12.5

Beta testing

A children's address book app holds the name and date of birth of each friend entered. It also takes as input, from the system, the current date. From these two data points it shows, as an output, the age of each friend.

For each of the data items, decide on:

a   the appropriate data type

b   appropriate validation that could be applied

c   invalid and, where appropriate, boundary data that could be used to test input validation.

SUMMARY

It is important to test systems to ensure they will perform as expected.
Alpha testing is completed during the programming of a system.
Beta testing is formal testing once the system has been completed.
Logical errors are errors in the logic of the process performed by the code. The code will run but will produce unexpected results. These need to be debugged manually using, for example, trace tables.
Syntax errors are errors in the syntax used within the code. It is likely that these will be identified by the IDE diagnostics.
Runtime errors only appear during the execution of the code. Attempting to divide by zero is a common runtime error.
IDEs identify syntax errors and runtime errors. IDEs also provide useful tools to help debug logical errors by providing the ability to step through code and add breakpoints.
Trace tables provide a useful means of tracing the value of variables, inputs, and outputs at each step of an algorithm. They can be helpful in identifying logical errors.
Valid data is met by the system in its normal operation.
Invalid data is data that the system is not expecting. The system should identify and reject invalid data and provide appropriate error messages.
Boundary data is data that falls at the extremes of a range of data. It is used to check the logic of the program at these extremes.

END-OF-CHAPTER TASKS

1 In the following two scenarios, say which is *alpha testing* and which is *beta testing*?

   a A programmer has completed programming the first level of a new game. She then runs some tests to check that her code is working before moving on to the other levels.

   b After completing a weather app, a software company sends early copies of the software to a group of people to try it out for a month and report back any problems they find.

2 In the following three scenarios, what are the most likely kinds of errors to look for: *logical errors, syntax errors* or *runtime errors*?

   a A program is undergoing beta testing and it is discovered that, after a little while, the program freezes because it has run out of allocated memory.

   b A program will refuse to run because of a missing speech mark.

   c A program is being written to calculate the total cost of products brought to a till at a supermarket. During alpha testing a strange thing is happening: No matter what products are in the basket, the total cost is $99.99.

3 In the three scenarios given in End-of-Chapter Task 2, what are the best ways of trying to diagnose and fix the problems encountered?

CONTINUED

4 The following algorithm is designed to accept a series of numbers in the range 0 to 100, with the sequence being ended by the user inputting a negative number. At the end of the sequence, the system will output the smallest number input, the largest number input, and the average of the numbers input. The algorithm contains eight logical errors. Identify the errors **and** explain how they could be corrected.

```
small ← 0
large ← 0
total ← 0
counter ← 0


INPUT number
WHILE number != -1 DO
    IF number > 0 OR number < 100
       THEN
         IF number < small
           THEN
              small ← number
         ENDIF
         IF number > large
           THEN
              number ← large
         ENDIF
         total ← total + number
         INPUT number
         counter = counter + 1
         average ← total / counter
         OUTPUT average
       ELSE
         OUTPUT 'Out of range - enter number'
         INPUT number
    ENDIF
ENDWHILE


OUTPUT 'small', large
```

5 Write a Python implementation of your corrected algorithm from End-of-Chapter Task 4.

Files and databases

Introduction

As you approach the end of this programming course, you will be very familiar with various ways of storing data in your programs. We have met constants, local and global variables and 2D and 3D arrays. These allow us to store data that may or may not change during the course of our programs. They enable us to store strings, Boolean data and various kinds of numbers both individually and in groups. However, all of the data stored in these systems are lost when the program is quit.

If you play a video game, you will not want to start from the beginning again every day. If your character has obtained the cloak of invisibility, you will expect to use it the next time you play. If the program stored this data in a variable, then when the program is quit all previous accomplishments will be lost. This is why many games have a Save Progress System. The achievements of that session of play are saved externally to the program, ready for loading up the next time the game is started.

An address book app that asked users to fill in the records every time it was started will not be very popular! Games and address books are examples of programs where there is a need to store data externally from the program. The two most common places for doing this are in files and databases.

13.1 Files

In the introduction, we thought about a game scenario that needs to store information about a character. In many games applications, the easiest way to do this is in files. Python, just like most modern programming languages, has the ability to read and write to text files and can do so in very sophisticated ways. For the syllabuses, we only need to know how to read or write a single item of data into and out of a file.

Reading files

The first task when reading data from a text file is to open it. This requires a bit of code that points to the file name and its location. Below is the pseudocode and Python code to do this:

Pseudocode:

```
my_file ← OPEN "my_file.txt"
```

Python code:

```
my_file = open('my_file.txt', 'r')
```

The 'r' parameter in the Python code indicates the way the file will be used: r stands for read, w for write.

Having opened the file, our program can now read the contents and assign it to a variable with Python's read() method:

Pseudocode:

```
my_file_data ← READ my_file
```

Python code:

```
my_file_data = my_file.read()
```

Now that the data is assigned to a variable our program can access the contents and use it in some way, such as output it:

Pseudocode:

```
OUTPUT my_text_data
```

Python code:

```
print(my_file_data)
```

Finally, it is important to remember to close the file to release memory resources back to the computer:

Pseudocode:

```
CLOSE my_file
```

Python code:

```
my_file.close()
```

Note that the file path is not required if the text file is stored in the same directory as the program script.

> **Further Information:**
>
> `read()` and `close()` are not functions. They are methods. Methods are a kind of function used in classes and objects. Classes and objects are used in Object Oriented Programming, or OOP, which is beyond the scope of this book. When calling methods, we use the dot operator after the object we are applying the method to, hence we write `my_file.close()` rather than `close(my_file)`.

Writing to files

The process is much the same as for reading except that when we open the file we use 'w' mode. The example below adds the text 'Tea time' to the file called `my_file.txt`:

Pseudocode:

```
my_file ← OPEN "my_file.txt"
WRITE "Tea time" TO my_file
CLOSE my_file
```

Code snippet 13.1

Python code:

```
my_file = open('my_file.txt', 'w')
my_file.write('Tea time')
my_file.close()
```

Code snippet 13.2

If the file with the provided filename does not already exist, Python will create one.

DEMO TASK 13.1

Name

Write a program that creates a file called name.txt *and then writes the text 'Red Rum' to the file and finally prints out 'The name of the horse is ' and adds the text from* name.txt.

Solution

Let's start planning this process in pseudocode:

```
name ← OPEN "name.txt"
WRITE "Red Rum" TO name
OUTPUT "The name of the horse is " + READ name
CLOSE name
```

Code snippet 13.3

CONTINUED

Although there are obviously a lot of easier ways to do this, we are following the instructions in this Demo Task. This will mean we can carefully examine what happens when we run our Python program. Here is the Python code that does the same thing as above (Code snippet 13.3):

```
# name.py
name = open('name.txt', 'w')
name.write('Red Rum')
name = open('name.txt', 'r')
print('The name of the horse is', name.read())
name.close()
```

Code snippet 13.4

PRACTICE TASKS 13.1–13.2

13.1 Name

a Write a new Python script called name.py and copy in Code snippet 13.4. Then save it and run it.

b Check that it produces the correct output in the Python shell but also look to see if it has created a text file called name.txt in the same directory as name.py.

c Open name.txt in your favourite text editor and look to see if the file contains the text 'Red Rum'.

13.2 Tuesday's weather

A weather app has been storing the temperatures every hour (from 6 a.m. to 6 p.m.) on a Tuesday. Tuesday's temperatures have been stored throughout the day in an array. Here are the contents of this array:

```
[4, 4, 8, 10, 14, 17, 19, 20, 20, 19, 17, 16, 14]
```

At the end of the day, this data needs to be written and saved to a text file.

a Write a pseudocode algorithm that initialises a list with the temperature data provided and then creates a file called tuesday.txt that contains a copy of the temperatures in one line of text. The temperatures must be stored in this form:

```
4,4,8,10,14,17,19,20,20,19,17,16,14
```

b Write and test a Python implementation of your algorithm.

Further Information:

Although it is useful to be able to open a file, read its contents and write to a text file, you may find yourself wanting to do other things. You may, for example, want to store more than just one piece of data in a file! Here are a few other things you may find handy when writing Python files:

Read every line of a text file into a list:

```
my_file = open('my_file.txt', 'r')
my_list = list(my_file)
```

Code snippet 13.5

Read and write a set of data into a file that is separated by spaces:

```
colours = open('colours.txt', 'w')
colours.write('Red Green Blue')
colours = open('colours.txt', 'r')
colours_list = colours.read().split()
print(colours_list[0]) # prints out 'Red'
colours.close()
```

Code snippet 13.6

CHALLENGE TASK 13.1

Names

Write a Python script called `names.py` and save it in the same directory as the `name.txt` file you made in Practice Task 13.1. In this script, write a program that reads in the contents of the text file and then prints out the following two lines of text:

First name: Red
Second name: Rum

Your program must use the data from `name.txt` to create these two lines of output. Instead of counting characters (the stored name might not always have the same number of letters as Red Rum) you can use Python's `split()` method which works like this:

```
>>> my_string = 'The cat sat on the mat'
>>> my_list = my_string.split()
>>> my_list
['The', 'cat', 'sat', 'on', 'the', 'mat']
>>>
```

13.2 Databases

A database is a collection of data stored in a logical and organised manner. It is worth reminding you that a paper-based address book is actually a database. There are, of course, also electronic databases. A shopping website will store all the photos, prices and other details of their products in an electronic database. Many web applications store their data in databases and use their system to provide personalised experiences for their users.

SQL stands for Structured Query Language. There are many different versions of this language produced by many vendors. In this chapter, you will be using SQLite. This is a simple and readily available database that is probably already installed on your computer and which works with Python well.

> ### KEY WORD
>
> SQL: Structured Query Language is a programming language used to manage and search databases.

> **Further Information:**
>
> A LAMP server is a common set-up for hosting interactive websites. It is made up from a server running the Linux operating system with Apache server software for hosting and distributing the websites. MySQL is the database programming language that reads, writes and maintains the database. PHP is the programming language that can talk to the HTML in the page and provide the logic in the system. PHP can send requests using the MySQL language to the database and process the output it receives. LAMP therefore stands for Linux Apache MySQL PHP; you might also see the terms WAMP, MAMP or XAMP which are Windows, MacOS and operating system independent versions of LAMP.
>
> There are many websites that replace PHP with Python or indeed other programming languages such as Java. These programming languages provide the logic capability for the system.

In the syllabuses, you are asked to learn about single-table databases. These are very easy to visualise. The first row of the table has column titles. Each title is the name of the field and the rows below are the records. So, rows contain records and columns contain fields. See Table 13.1 for an example of a single-table database.

> ### KEY WORDS
>
> field: a column of data held in a database table.
>
> record: a row of data held in a database table.

Record ID	Player alias	Invisibility Cloak	Speed	Strength	Sprite
1	Sirra	0	7	2	Elf
2	Hagor	0	3	7	Giant
3	Flydart	1	3	3	Human
4	Grissle	0	6	3	Elf
5	Jaws	0	2	8	Giant

Table 13.1: A single-table database

Primary key

Databases can be huge, and are stored electronically. For the information in the different records to be accessed accurately each record (row in the table) needs at least one piece of data to be unique. The field with unique data for each record is called the primary key. When preparing for exams, you may get asked to suggest which field could be used as the primary key. In practice, most programmers would add an ID to every record as the primary key to ensure that there is a way of uniquely identifying every record. In fact when SQL is used to create a table it can do this for you.

> ### KEY WORD
>
> primary key: a field in a database table that holds unique values that can be used to identify each record in the table.

PRACTICE TASK 13.3

Primary key

If there was not a Record ID in Table 13.1, which field could be used as the primary key for this database table?

Data types and validation

So that the data stored in a database is searchable and can be efficiently used in programs, the data in the fields has to be of only one type. The data types for each field are defined when the empty table is created. The data types (Table 13.2) are very similar to those found in Python:

SQL Data Type	SQLite	Python Equivalent
text/alphanumeric	text	String
character	Use text	String
Boolean	Use 0 and 1 as integers	Boolean
integer	integer	Int
real	real	Float
date/time	(Use text or integers)	(needs the datetime module to be imported)

Table 13.2: Database data types

PRACTICE TASK 13.4

Boolean data

In Table 13.1, the data types being used are those available in an SQLite database. Which fields are being stored as Boolean values?

Databases are also able to employ validation on the data entered in a very similar way to that described for Python in Chapter 11. The simplest form of this validation is checking whether the data being entered matches the data type defined for the field. One other important validation process can be run and that is to check that a new primary key entry is unique. Programming validation in SQL is beyond the scope of the syllabuses.

13.3 Querying databases

This is an interesting chapter because, not only are we learning how to store data externally from our programs, but we are also seeing how two very different programming languages can 'talk' to each other. This does mean you must learn a small amount of another programming language. However, this is not too difficult as you do not have to learn too much and SQL is a **declarative language**. (Declarative languages are those where the programmer declares what the program has to do but leaves it up to the language to find the most efficient way of doing this.) Nonetheless, the programmer does have to ask precisely and unambiguously for what is required and must use the SQL keywords accurately.

You are going to learn how to use these keywords in your queries:

SELECT, FROM, WHERE, ORDER BY, SUM, COUNT.

Introducing the Python Database Tool

To help you practise writing some SQL queries, a Python Database Tool (see Figure 13.1) has been produced to accompany this book. It can be found on the digital part of this resource on Cambridge GO. After unzipping the PythonDatabaseTool.zip folder, you will find it contains a Python script, two images and two database files (identifiable by their .db file extension). It is best to keep this folder as it is or make a copy of the complete folder. This is because the databases you will make and the images required by the application all need to be in the same folder for it to work.

KEY WORD

declarative language: a programming language where precise instructions are written in a program but the language looks after how this is achieved.

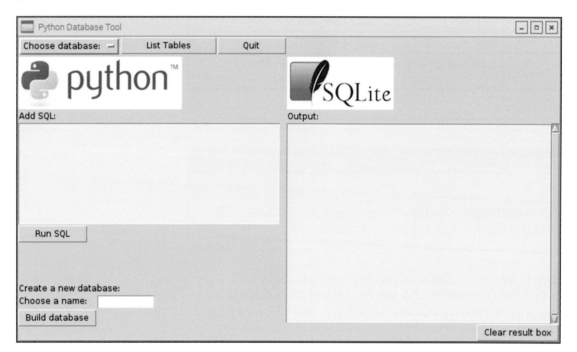

Figure 13.1: The Python Database Tool

To run the tool, simply open `database_tool.py` and run as normal. The script is a little longer than you are used to but you are welcome to look through it! This application and how it was created will be discussed a little later in this chapter in optional sections 13.4 and 13.5.

Using the Python Database Tool

The first thing to do is to load a database. To do this, select the `characters` database from the *Choose database* drop-down menu. Now to check everything is in order and to see the whole table, enter the following code into the Add SQL text box on the left:

```
SELECT * FROM Character;
```

(Note: The database is called `characters` and the table is called `Character`.)

If all is well, after pressing the 'Run SQL' button, you should see the following output:

```
+--------------------------------------------------------------------+
| RecordID | Player_alias | Invis_cloak | Speed | Strength | Sprite |
+--------------------------------------------------------------------+
| 1        | Sirra        | 0           | 7     | 2        | Elf    |
| 2        | Hagor        | 0           | 3     | 7        | Giant  |
| 3        | Flydart      | 1           | 3     | 3        | Human  |
| 4        | Grissle      | 0           | 6     | 3        | Elf    |
| 5        | Jaws         | 0           | 2     | 8        | Giant  |
+--------------------------------------------------------------------+
```

PRACTICE TASK 13.5

Book table

Use the tool to show the whole of the `Book` table from the `books` database (this is also supplied with the tool).

Writing SQL queries

In the tasks in the rest of this section of the chapter, you are going to use the Python Database Tool to write SQL queries similar to those you could be asked to perform in an examination. Remember that if you get into a mess with it, you can effectively reset it by quitting and re-running `database_tool.py`.

KEY WORD

query: a question asked of a database when using the SQL language.

PRACTICE TASK 13.6

Resetting

Why does quitting and restarting the Python Database Tool reset everything?

SQL does not take any notice of capitalisation. However, it is a convention that, for ease of reading, the SQL command words are capitalised. It is also a good idea to start a new line for each new criteria being applied to a search. Some SQL databases require a semi-colon at the end of each query. This is not required in SQLite with simple single SQL queries, but we will use semi-colons anyway so that our queries could be used with any SQL database.

Table 13.3 provides you with the main SQL keywords you will use. In addition to these, SQL can also use all the normal logic operators you are familiar with; e.g. =, >=, !=, AND, OR and NOT.

Keyword	Meaning	Notes
SELECT	This command initiates a search of the database.	The Python Database Tool looks for this word and then applies some special formatting to the output.
FROM	Specifies the table that will be searched.	
WHERE	Specifies the field that the criteria applies to.	There can be more than one criteria.
ORDER BY	Specifies the field that the results should be used to sort the output by.	This command always has to be at the end of your query. Use the keyword ASC to indicate your sort should be ascending (e.g. A–Z or 1–9) and DESC to indicate you want the results in descending order (e.g. Z–A or 9–1).
SUM	Finds the total of all items in a specified field.	SELECT SUM(fieldname) FROM tablename
COUNT	Finds the number of items in a specified field.	SELECT COUNT(fieldname) FROM tablename
;	The end of an SQL query.	Semi-colons are normally required at the end of blocks of code in SQL.
*	A symbol that means 'everything'.	This saves us having to list out a whole set of criteria if we just want to see all the data.

Table 13.3: SQL keywords

DEMO TASK 13.2

Tolkien's books after 1940

Perform a search of the books.db *database to find all the books written by Tolkien after 1940. The output should be arranged in order of year of publication, starting with the most recent at the top. Do not include the BookID field.*

Solution

First the table needs to be selected, so the query will start with something like:

```
SELECT * FROM Book
```

This will select all the fields though, so this needs to be amended to only include the fields requested:

```
SELECT Title, Author, Year FROM Book
```

Next, a WHERE clause is required to indicate that only results from Tolkien and after 1940 are required:

```
WHERE Author = 'Tolkien' AND Year > 1940
```

Finally, the ORDER clause needs to stipulate that the results should be presented in Year order and descending numerically:

```
ORDER BY Year DESC;
```

CONTINUED

The final query and the output can be seen in Figure 13.2:

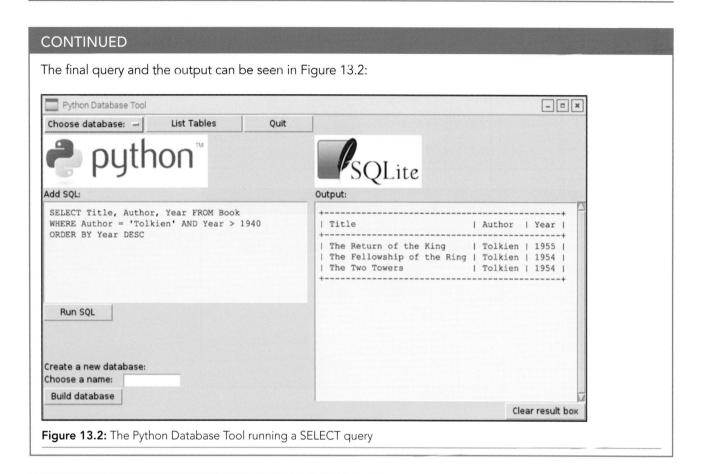

Figure 13.2: The Python Database Tool running a SELECT query

PRACTICE TASK 13.7

Perform a search of the books.db database to do the following:

a   Show the complete Book table with the books published earliest at the top.

b   Show all books published by Orwell in alphabetical order.

c   Show all the books in order of publication. Your output should only show the Title and Author of the books.

d   Show the complete Book table, leaving out the BookID field. The output should be sorted first by author alphabetically and then by title alphabetically.

e   Show all rows in the Book table with the books published most recently at the top. Only show three fields, which should be displayed in the order Author, Title, Year from left to right.

f   Show all the books in order of publication. Your results should only show books published between the years 1940 and 1950.

TIP

For Task 13.7d, you can list several ORDER BY criteria separated by commas.

PRACTICE TASK 13.8

Perform a search of the characters.db database to do the following:

a   Output the sum of the speeds of all characters.

b   Output the total strength of all the Giants.

c   Output the number of Elves in the database.

CHALLENGE TASK 13.2

Perform a search of the characters.db database that outputs the total speed and total strength of the Giants in the database. The output should look like this:

```
+----------------------------+
| SUM(Speed)  | SUM(Strength) |
+----------------------------+
| 5           | 15            |
+----------------------------+
```

Note: Section 13.4 is optional. It goes beyond what you need to know for the syllabuses.

13.4 Python and SQL

We are now going to look at how the Python Database Tool was built and, in so doing, see an example of an application that uses two programming languages (Python and SQL) to create an application.

To start this section, open the database_tool.py in your IDE and look through the code. Look for things you recognise.

There are several things you should recognise:

- It has plenty of comments and is organised in the usual way, keeping design separate from functionality.

- We import several Python modules but only one is imported in a way such that we can write our function calls without using the module name.

- There are some global variables declared and initialised at the start.

- There are several functions with descriptive names.

- Finally, we build our GUI design.

Once you have looked through the code to see how label widgets can be used to display images, you should see that, given enough time, you would have been able to produce the GUI part of the application yourself. Note that before images can be used by a widget, it is necessary to load them into memory using the tkinter `PhotoImage()` function. All of the GUI code is found below the `#### main:` comment.

Examining the rest of the code, you will find that there are quite a number of functions. They have been organised into two groups: **(i)** those that are called by the buttons and the drop-down menu, **(ii)** several utility functions. Studying the code in these functions should enable you to see that this application has been built using the same techniques of top-down design and algorithm implementation taught in the rest of the book. Interestingly, you will find it difficult to find where Python and SQL interact. This is because this is a Python program and it is the users who provide the majority of the SQL. The `run_sql()` function is where you can see the interaction between the two languages. The SQL queries entered by the user are passed to this function as a string and then a connection is made to the database. The query is then executed and then there is a `db.commit` command that saves the result to the database file.

There is one utility function that is rather long called `pretty_tables()`. You are not intended to be able to follow this entirely as it uses several more complex methods that are available in Python for navigating through the container variables. There is some slicing of strings and iterating through the list of tuples output from the database. All you need to know is that it reformats the output from searches into neat tables. (Tuples are efficient container data types that are read in the same way as lists but that cannot have their contents changed.)

> **Note:** Section 13.5 is optional. It goes beyond what you need to know for the syllabuses.

13.5 More advanced SQL

This section uses some of the other facilities in the Python Database Tool that allow you to create your own database and tables, and populate them.

Rather than explain how this application works, you will be learning by doing. In this section, you are going to dive straight in with some tasks that will help you get familiar with this SQL learning tool.

PRACTICE TASKS 13.9–13.11

13.9 Create a new database

    a   Open and run database_tool.py then, using the **Create a new database** tool, add the name 'trees' to the **Choose a name** textbox and click **Build database**.

    b   Find the file you have created called trees.db on your computer. Where is it found?

    c   Select this database. It should now be available to you in the **Choose database** drop-down menu.

CONTINUED

13.10 Build a table

a   Open and run database_tool.py then select your trees.db database from the **Choose database** drop-down menu.

b   In the **Add SQL** textbox enter the following code and then press **Run SQL**:

```
CREATE TABLE Tree(
    TreeID integer,
    Name text,
    Fruit text,
    Year_planted integer,
    Primary Key(TreeID));
```

If all is well, [] will appear in the output window and no errors will be produced.

c   Look again at the *Python Database Tool*. How else can you find out if you have successfully added a table?

13.11 Populate the table

a   Open and run database_tool.py then select your trees.db database from the **Choose database** drop-down menu.

b   In the **Add SQL** textbox enter the following lines of SQL one at a time pressing **Run SQL** after each entry.

```
INSERT INTO Tree (Name, Fruit, Year_planted)
VALUES ('Braeburn','Apple',1999);


INSERT INTO Tree (Name, Fruit, Year_planted)
VALUES ('Bountiful','Apple',2001);


INSERT INTO Tree (Name, Fruit, Year_planted)
VALUES ('Avalon Pride','Peach',2017);


INSERT INTO Tree (Name, Fruit, Year_planted)
VALUES ('Jenny','Kiwi',2020);
```

If all is well, [] will appear in the output window and no errors will be produced each time you press the **Run SQL** button.

c   Check everything is OK by typing in `SELECT * FROM Tree;` What does the asterisk represent?

d   Add one of the book entries a second time, check it is added twice and then delete it with the following SQL:

```
DELETE FROM Tree WHERE BookID = 5;
```

SUMMARY

Programs that need to store data that is saved after the program is quit can save their data in files or databases.
Programs can open and close a named text file.
Once a program has opened a file, the data can be read in and assigned to a variable for further processing.
Computer programs can also write data into existing text files or create new ones.
A database is a collection of data stored in a logical and ordered manner. Databases can be paper based or electronic.
Data in databases is stored in tables consisting of records and fields.
A record is a collection of data about one single item in a database. It corresponds to a row in a table.
A field is one piece of data about an item in a database. In a table, the field information for each record is displayed in the same column.
Each database field must be given a data type.
Databases can validate new data before it is entered.
Tables need a primary key. This is a field that holds data that uniquely identifies a record.
A search for data in a database is known as a 'query'.
SQL is a programming language that is used to maintain databases and run queries.
Python's SQLite3 library provides tools that allow Python to perform SQL queries in a simple database and process the output.

END-OF-CHAPTER TASKS

1 a   Write a program in pseudocode that creates a file called `birthday.txt` and then writes the text '25th May 2009' to the file and finally prints out 'I was born on ' and adds the text from `birthday.txt`.

   b   Write a Python implementation of your pseudocode program and test everything works as it should.

2 a   Write the pseudocode for a procedure called `update_leaderboard()` that creates a file called leader.txt and enters your name as the value. Don't forget to close your file.

   b   Write a text-based Python implementation of your pseudocode algorithm and test it works as it should.

3 a   Write the pseudocode for a procedure called `get_leader()` that opens the file called leader.txt created in task 2 and reads the contents of the file and assigns it to a variable called 'leader'. Your program should then print out: 'Today's leader is: ' followed by the name stored in the file.

   b   Write a text-based Python implementation of your pseudocode algorithm and test it works as it should.

4 a   Perform a search of the characters.db database to show the complete `Character` table.

   b   Write down the SQL code you used.

CONTINUED

5 a Perform a search of the character.db database to show all information about the Giants.

   b Write down the SQL code you used.

6 a Perform a search of the characters.db database to show only the name, speed and strength of the characters.

   b Write down the SQL code you used.

7 a Perform a search of the books.db database that counts the number of books it contains written by Orwell.

   b Write down the SQL code you used.

> Chapter 14
Programming scenario task

IN THIS CHAPTER YOU WILL:

- analyse problems to create programming solutions
- understand how to tackle a large problem
- identify the inputs, processes and outputs of a problem
- use pseudocode or program code to write solutions for problems.

The information in this chapter is based on the Cambridge IGCSE, IGCSE (9–1) and O Level Computer Science syllabuses (0478/0984/2210) for examination from 2023. You should always refer to the appropriate syllabus document for the year of your examination to confirm the details and for more information. The syllabus documents are available on the Cambridge International website at www.cambridgeinternational.org

Introduction

This chapter supports the 'programming scenario task' in the new syllabuses. The chapter will take you through a demo task in the style of a programming scenario task and will provide step-by-step suggestions of how to break the task down and construct an appropriate solution. This task will require you to write a program in either pseudocode or program code. You will need to use many of the programming techniques you have learned while working through the book. If there are areas that you don't understand, it might help to re-visit the relevant section of the book. You shouldn't worry about providing a perfect solution for these types of task.

14.1 Reading the question

It would be great to be able to read the question, decompose it and produce a structure diagram, then a flowchart, write some pseudocode, and finally write the program and test it. However, there is not enough time to do all of this. To develop an efficient system for answering these questions, you will need to draw on aspects from these planning skills but some shortcuts will be necessary. Whether you are going to provide a Python or pseudocode solution, it is recommended that you break the scenario down into just three areas:

- inputs
- processes
- outputs.

The **inputs** are to be found in the question text somewhere; you may even be given variable names that you must use. Highlight them in the question in some way. (Underline them or use a highlighter pen.)

The **processes** should also be fully described in the question text. However, although this is where much of the work is going to be required, leave this for the moment.

The required **outputs** should be carefully described in the question. This is what your processes have to produce, so highlight these in the question text as well – perhaps in a different colour.

> ### KEY WORDS
>
> **input:** data that is required by a program to complete the required task. The data can be obtained from the user, a file or database, a device or another program.
>
> **process:** a part of a program where the input data is used to complete the required task.
>
> **output:** textual, visual or audio data that is produced by a program. The output can be sent to an output device, stored in a file or database or displayed to a user.

DEMO TASK 14.1

Washing machine program

An automatic washing machine contains a small computer that controls the operation of the machine. The user has to identify the type of load for the wash. Examples of types of load are white cotton, cotton colours and wool. The type of load has to be chosen so that appropriate controls can be set for the wash. Table 14.1 shows the five features that have to be controlled together with the range of possible values that can be chosen.

CONTINUED

Features to be controlled	wash time (in mins)	agitation speed	wash temperature (in °C)	rinse time (in mins)	rinse speed (1 to 10)
Minimum value	10	01	20	05	01
Maximum value	70	10	90	30	10

Table 14.1: Variables in the washing machine program

The program running the machine has access to a number of text files. Each text file contains a list of values for one type of load. The name of each text file matches the name of a particular type of load. The line of text in each text file has five two-digit numbers separated by single spaces.

For example, the text file `wools.txt` *contains:*

`30 02 30 30 02`

The requirements for the part of the program that you are asked to write are as follows:

- *The name for the type of load is input (e.g. 'wools').*
- *The control data for this load is read from the appropriate file (e.g.* `wools.txt`*).*
- *The data from the file is split into five values.*
- *The data for the wash temperature is checked to ensure that it is within the allowed range.*
- *If the temperature is not in the allowed range, the program sends an error message and stops.*
- *The total time for the wash is calculated and output in hours and minutes.*
- *The wash temperature is output.*
- *The text file is closed.*

Solution

The inputs mentioned in the question have been highlighted in yellow, and the required outputs have been highlighted in blue. In addition, the request to close the file where the data is stored has been highlighted in pink. The question kindly reminds us to do this but do be aware that this is something you should always do, whether instructed to or not.

Note that we may not have identified all the variables we will need, but we have made a start. This is not the whole solution! As this is an extended task, the rest of this chapter describes how to go about completing a full solution to this scenario task.

14.2 Constructing a skeleton answer

At this early stage, we can set out a list of comments separated by plenty of space to allow code to be inserted between them. We might also add some simple code such as the inputs and anything we do not want to forget. Our plan, after completing this stage, might look like the following (but with more space between the comments):

```
# Input the load type
load_type = input('Input washing program: ')


# Open and read text file


# Split file data and then assign values to five variables
wash_time =
agitation_speed =
wash_temp =
rinse_time =
rinse_speed =


# Check the temperature is in range

    # Calculate the total wash program time (if temp OK)

    # Required outputs (duration, wash temperature) (if temp OK)

# Close the file
file.close()
```

Code snippet 14.1

TIP

As you work through the development of the solution to this demo task, it is a good idea to build your own solution along with the explanation so that at the end of the process you have either a full pseudocode answer or a working Python program.

14.3 Filling in the details

Presenting our plan as comments gives us a framework for writing our code, but also starts the process of properly commenting our program. We do not have to fill in the missing code by starting at the beginning and working through to the end. We can start by writing the code for the parts of our program with which we are most confident. This will be particularly sensible if you are short of time when answering a question like this.

Opening and reading the content from the file is just a syntax problem. In Python it is done like this:

```
# Input the selected load type
load_type = input('Input washing program: ')


# Open and read text file
filename = load_type + '.txt'
file = open(filename, 'r')
file_data = file.read()
```

Code snippet 14.2

and in pseudocode it is done like this:

```
// Input the selected program as a string
load_type ← INPUT
```

```
// Open and read text file
filename ← load_type + '.txt'
file ← OPEN filename
file_data ← READ file
```

Code snippet 14.3

The first process we have to solve is how to go about splitting the text string that is currently held in the variable file_data. This needs splitting into the five required variables. In pseudocode we can use SUBSTRING() like this:

```
// Split file_data and assign values to 5 integer variables
wash_time ← INTEGER(SUBSTRING(file_data, 1, 2))
agitation_speed ← INTEGER(SUBSTRING(file_data, 4, 2))
wash_temp ← INTEGER(SUBSTRING(file_data, 7, 2))
rinse_time ← INTEGER(SUBSTRING(file_data, 10, 2))
rinse_speed ← INTEGER(SUBSTRING(file_data, 13, 2))
```

Code snippet 14.4

We could do the same thing in Python but a more common way is to use the built-in split() method like this:

```
# Split file_data into a list and assign values to 5 variables
data = file_data.split()
wash_time = int(data[0])
agitation_speed = int(data[1])
wash_temp = int(data[2])
rinse_time = int(data[3])
rinse_speed = int(data[4])
```

Code snippet 14.5

Calculating the total wash duration will take two steps: First, we add the wash_time and rinse_time. Then we use modulus division to find the hours and minutes. In Python, this is achieved like this:

```
# Calculate the total wash program time (if temp OK)
minutes = wash_time + rinse_time
duration = str(minutes // 60) + 'hours ' + str(minutes % 60) + 'mins'
```

Code snippet 14.6

and in pseudocode it is done like this:

```
// Calculate the total wash program time (if temp OK)
minutes ← wash_time + rinse_time
duration ← STRING(minutes DIV 60) + 'hours ' + STRING(minutes MOD 60) + 'mins'
```

Code snippet 14.7

Finally, we produce the required output. In pseudocode this is achieved like this:

```
// Required outputs (if temp OK)
OUTPUT 'Program duration: ' + duration
OUTPUT 'Wash temperature: ' + STRING(wash_temp) + 'oC')
```

Code snippet 14.8

and in Python:

```
# Calculate the total wash program time (if temp OK)
print('Program duration:', duration)
print('Wash temperature: ' + str(wash_temp) + 'oC')
```

Code snippet 14.9

Note that we have skipped the validation of the temperature until this stage. When we wrote our skeleton structure, we left room for this by indenting the comments for the code that only runs if the temperature is in range. It is now easy to wrap these indented code blocks in our IF statements. This can be seen in the next section.

14.4 Putting it all together

Here is the full solution for the washing machine program scenario, first in Python and then in pseudocode:

A Python solution:

```
# Input the selected program as a string
load_type = input('Input washing program: ')

# Open and read text file
filename = load_type + '.txt'
file = open(filename, 'r')
file_data = file.read()

# Split file_data into a list and assign values to 5 variables
data = file_data.split()
wash_time = int(data[0])
agitation_speed = int(data[1])
wash_temp = int(data[2])
rinse_time = int(data[3])
rinse_speed = int(data[4])

# Check the temperature is in range before calculations
if wash_temp < 20 or wash_temp > 90:
    print('Program error.')
else:
    # Calculate the total wash program time
    minutes = wash_time + rinse_time
    duration = str(minutes // 60) + 'hours ' + str(minutes % 60) + 'mins'
    # Required outputs
    print('Program duration:', duration)
    print('Wash temperature: ' + str(wash_temp) + 'oC')

# Close the file
file.close()
```

Code snippet 14.10

A pseudocode solution:

```
// Input the selected program as a string
load_type ← INPUT

// Open and read text file
filename ← load-type + '.txt'
file ← OPEN filename
file_data ← READ file

// Split file_data and assign values to 5 integer variables
wash_time ← INTEGER(SUBSTRING(file_data, 1, 2))
agitation_speed ← INTEGER(SUBSTRING(file_data, 4, 2))
wash_temp ← INTEGER(SUBSTRING(file_data, 7, 2))
rinse_time ← INTEGER(SUBSTRING(file_data, 10, 2))
rinse_speed ← INTEGER(SUBSTRING(file_data, 13, 2))

// Check the temperature is in range before calculations
IF wash_temp < 20 OR wash_temp > 90
  THEN
    OUTPUT 'Program error.'
  ELSE
    // Calculate and the total wash program time
    minutes ← wash_time + rinse_time
    duration ← STRING(minutes DIV 60) + 'hours ' + STRING(minutes MOD 60) + 'mins'
    // Required outputs
    OUTPUT 'Program duration: ' + duration
    OUTPUT 'Wash temperature: ' + STRING(wash_temp) + 'oC')
ENDIF

// Close the file
CLOSE file
```

Code snippet 14.11

14.5 Final thoughts

Once you have finished what you can, it is useful to go through a mental checklist to try to ensure you get as many of the marks available as possible. Table 14.2 shows a suggested checklist:

Variables	• Have I used the variable names provided?
	• Are my own variable names meaningful?
	• Are my variables all of the correct data type?
Inputs	• Have I included effective validation for all inputs?

(continued)

Processes	• Are my algorithmic solutions efficient?
	• Have I used appropriate loops?
	• Are the data structures I have used in my algorithms the best ones to use?
	• Do my data structures store all the data they should?
Outputs	• Does my program produce all the outputs required?
	• Are the outputs in the form asked for?
Other	• Is my solution properly commented?

Table 14.2: Mental checklist

If you have worked through the first 13 chapters of this book, you already have all the programming techniques necessary to answer these types of questions. The best way to develop your skills is to practise with the end-of-chapter tasks. Feel free to look back at some of the suggestions and strategies provided in this chapter and to use the checklist in Table 14.2 before practising a task like this. Time yourself to see how long it takes but do not worry if at first you are taking a longer than 30 minutes.
As you do more of these types of questions, you will get faster.

SUMMARY

Identify the inputs, processes and outputs of the scenario.
Use appropriate messages when inputting and outputting data.
Create a structured plan using commenting.
Use meaningful identifiers for variables, constants and subroutines.
Select appropriate data types if not provided.
Choose efficient algorithms for processing data.
Ensure outputs are in the form requested.
Add further comments to explain your code, if necessary.

END-OF-CHAPTER TASKS

The end-of-chapter tasks provided here require similar approaches to the demo challenge you have just studied. Some are easier than others. By completing them all, you will have used a range of different programming techniques. You will find solutions provided in both pseudocode and Python. After you have produced your own solution to a task, compare your solution with the corresponding one provided. See if there is anything you have missed out or that is done in a better way before moving on to the next task.

CONTINUED

For all of the following tasks you should:

- provide a pseudocode or Python answer
- add comments to explain how your code works.

1 A game program is needed for two players that finds out which player is the best guesser:

Player 1 is invited to play.

Player 1 is asked to guess a number between 1 and 10. The input value is compared to a randomly generated number. If the numbers match, the score for Player 1 is incremented. The process is repeated for Player 1 another nine times.

Player 2 is invited to play.

There is a repeat of the guessing of ten numbers by Player 2.

The scores for the two players are compared. The winner is the player with the highest score.

If the scores are the same, the game is drawn.

The program should output the identity of the winner or a string indicating that the game was drawn.

2 The 1D array `SnackName[]` contains the names of popular sweetshop snacks. The 2D array `Nutrition[]` contains the mass (in grams per 100 g) of carbohydrates, sugars, protein and salt for each snack. (The sugars are a subset of the carbohydrates.) The index values for the rows in the 2D array match the indexes in the 1D array; for example, the snack in index position 2 in `SnackName[]` is Chocbar and its data is stored in index position 2 in `Nutrition[]`.

`SnackName` array:

Index:	0	1	2	3	4
Name:	Caramello	Oaty	Chocbar	Slimaid	Nutter

`Nutrition` array:

Index	Carbohydrate /100 g	Sugars /100 g	Protein /100 g	Salt /100 g
0	69.3	59.9	4.4	0.42
1	65.1	32.3	5.1	0.48
2	59.8	58.7	5.8	0.2
3	35.4	27.1	3.1	0.32
4	54.4	44.8	9.9	0.45

The variable `SampleSize` contains the number of snacks in the system. All snacks contain data on the same four ingredients.

The arrays and variables have already been set up and the data stored. Snacks are awarded a grade based on the following calculation:

`HealthIndex` = Carbohydrate + (Sugars * 2) + (Salt * 100)

There are three Health Ratings:

- Red = `HealthIndex` that is 200 or above
- Orange = `HealthIndex` that is 150 to 199
- Green = `HealthIndex` less than 150.

CONTINUED

Write a program that meets the following requirements:

- Calculates the `HealthIndex` for all snacks.

- Calculates the average `HealthIndex` for all the snacks, rounded to the nearest whole number.

- Outputs, for each snack:

  - name

  - percentage of snack that is carbohydrates, rounded to the nearest whole number

  - `HealthIndex`

  - health rating (Red, Orange, Green).

- Calculates, stores and outputs the number of red, orange and green snacks there are in the whole sample and the average `HealthIndex`.

You do **not** need to declare or initialise the data in the provided arrays.

3 A bank is developing a system for handling interactions with customers. The system will contain a suite of individual programs. You are requested to provide a program for checking the `customerID` when a customer logs in. The program requirement is as follows:

- The program will begin by requesting input of the `customerID` from the customer.

- A correct `customerID` consists of four lower case letters followed by two numeric digits.

- The program will check that the input matches this required format.

- This will require three checks:

  - that the length of the input string is six

  - that the first four characters are lower case letters

  - that the last two characters are numeric digits.

- If a check finds an error, the program must output a message indicating the type of error that has been found.

- Following this error message, the customer is offered the chance to input the `customerID` again.

- The customer will only be allowed three attempts.

- If three incorrect attempts have been entered, the program will output a message to state that no further attempts will be allowed.

- If a customer has entered a `customerID` in the correct format, the program ends by outputting a message to say that the input has been accepted.

4 A 1D array `Members[]` contains the name of 50 members of a running club. All members of the club have taken part in a competition. The distance each member ran in 30 minutes was recorded. A 2D array `Distance[]` contains the distance, in metres, for each run, for each member. It was possible for members to have three attempts at the run but not all members completed three runs. The value −1 has been recorded where the member did not complete a run. The position of each member's data in the arrays is the same. For example, the member at position 20 in the array `Members[]` will have their runs recorded at position 20 in the array `Distance[]`.

The arrays have already been set up and the data stored.

Members are allocated categories based on the distance achieved in their best run.

CONTINUED

Category	Distance achieved in best run
Elite	Greater than or equal to 7 kilometres
Championship	Greater than or equal to 5 kilometres and less than 7 kilometres
Club	Less than 5 kilometres

Write a program that meets the following requirements:

- Calculates the average distance run for each member. Where a member has completed fewer than three runs, the average will be based only on the number of runs, they completed.

- Calculates the best distance for each member.

- Output, for each member:

  - name

  - number of runs completed

  - average distance covered

  - best distance

  - category awarded.

- Calculates, stores and outputs the total distance ran in the competition.

You must use pseudocode or programming code and add comments to explain how your code works.

You do **not** need to declare or initialise the data in the provided arrays.

5   A 1D array `Schools[]` contains the names of 30 schools taking part in a weather monitoring project. The project lasts for 7 days. Each school records both the minimum and the maximum temperature, in Celsius, at their location for each of the 7 days. The 2D array `MinTemp[]` contains the minimum temperature recorded at each school for each of the 7 days. The 2D array `MaxTemp[]` contains the maximum temperature recorded at each school for each of the 7 days. The position of each school's data in the three arrays is the same.

The arrays and variables have already been set up and the data stored.

Write a program that meets the following requirements:

- Calculates the daily temperature range (maximum temperature minus minimum temperature) for each of the schools.

- Calculates the average daily temperature range over the 7-day period for each school.

- Calculates the average maximum temperature over the 7-day period for each school.

- Outputs, for each school:

  - name

  - average temperature range

  - average maximum temperature.

- Calculates, stores and outputs the highest temperature and the lowest temperature recorded at any of the schools.

You do **not** need to declare or initialise the data in the provided arrays.

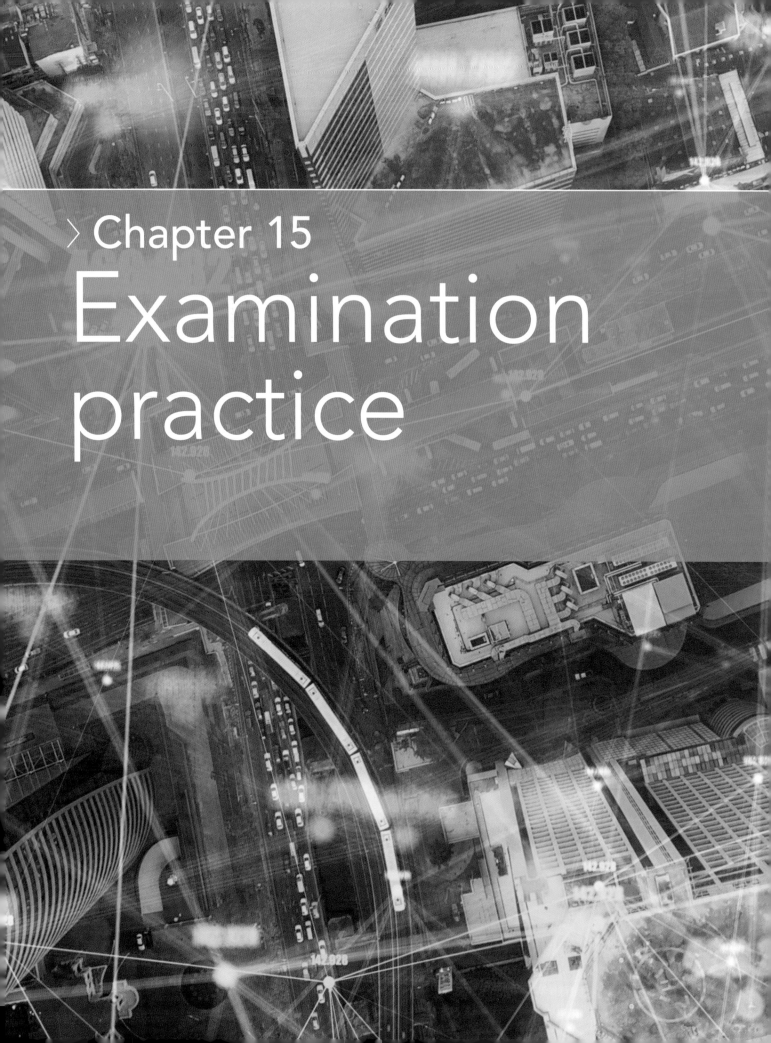

> Chapter 15
Examination practice

Exam-style questions and mark scheme guidance have been written by the authors. In examinations, the way marks are awarded may be different. References to assessment and/or assessment preparation are the publisher's interpretation of the syllabus requirements and may not fully reflect the approach of Cambridge Assessment International Education.

Introduction

This chapter includes a series of exam-style questions. This chapter aims to bring together all the skills you have developed and all the knowledge you have gained throughout this book. The questions will test your understanding of key programming concepts you have learned and offer you an opportunity to identify any gaps in your understanding. If you are unsure about how to answer a particular question, it may help to re-visit the relevant section of the book. There are full, suggested solutions in the solutions chapter in the digital part of this resource. Remember that there is often more than one solution. Good luck!

EXAM-STYLE QUESTIONS

1   A school is holding a vote to decide on the name for a new science block. The two options are Faraday and Curie. Each of the 601 students will vote. An algorithm is to be created for an electronic voting system that will record the vote of each student. You can assume that all the students will make a valid vote. The system will output the most popular name and the percentage of students that voted for that name.

    Write an algorithm for the voting system, using pseudocode or a flowchart.

[6]

2   The pseudocode below inputs the scores achieved by students in a test. The maximum score in the test was 200, A value of −1 stops the input. The algorithm outputs the highest, lowest and average score.

```
INT: Marks ← 0
INT High ← 0
INT Low ← 0
INT Total ← 0
INT Count ← 0
REAL Average ← 0


PRINT "Enter Student Marks"
INPUT Marks
WHILE Marks <> -1 DO
    Total ← Total + Marks
    Count ← Count + 1
    IF Marks <= High
      THEN
         High ← Marks
       ELSE IF Marks < Low
         Marks ← Low
    ENDIF
    PRINT "Enter Student Marks"
    INPUT Marks
ENDWHILE
Average ← Count / Total
PRINT High, Low, Average
```

CONTINUED

There are four errors in the algorithm.

Locate those errors and show how the error could be corrected.

[8]

3 A system accepts 13-digit ISBN numbers. The ISBN number includes a check digit.

   a Explain how a check digit is used to validate the input

[4]

   b The pseudocode has been written to complete other types of validation.
For each example state the what type of validation is being completed.

Pseudocode	Type of validation
```INPUT ISBN IF ISBN = "" THEN PRINT "Error" ENDIF```	
```INPUT ISBN IF Len(ISBN) < 13 THEN PRINT "Error" ENDIF```	

[2]

   c This pseudocode has been written to validate user input for a system that accepts only integer values.

```
INT: UserValue
INPUT UserValue
WHILE UserValue <=10 OR UserInput > 200 DO
    OUTPUT "Out of range, re-enter value"
    INPUT UserValue
ENDWHILE
```

The code is to be tested using normal, abnormal and extreme data.

Give one example of each type of test data (Normal, Abnormal and Extreme) that could be used to test the validation algorithm.

[3]

[Total: 9]

4 The algorithm inputs a series of integer values. A negative value stops the input.

```
INT: Number ← 0
INT Count ← 0
INT Total ← 0
INT Large ← 0
REPEAT
    INPUT Number
    Count ← Count + 1
    IF Number > 10
      THEN
```

CONTINUED

```
            Total ← Total + Number
            IF Total MOD 20 = 0
              THEN
                 Large = Total DIV 20
            ENDIF
        ENDIF

UNTIL Number < 0
Count ← Count -1
OUTPUT Large * Count
```

Create and complete the trace table for the following sequence of inputs:

15, 10, 14, 0, 12, 19, 11, −6.

Use the following headings:

Number	Count	Total	Large	Output

[5]

5   An array `Netname` holds the network username of 600 employees. The array has not been sorted.

An algorithm is required that will search the array for a specific username. If the username is in the array the algorithm will output the index location of the array that holds the specific username. If the username is not in the array the algorithm will output the message "No Record".

a   Write the search algorithm, using pseudocode or a flowchart.

[5]

The array `Netname` has been sorted in alphabetical ascending order.

b   Explain how your algorithm could be made more efficient now the array `Netname` is sorted.

[3]

[Total: 8]

6   A two-dimensional array is used in an electronic board game. The pseudocode to declare the array is:

```
Board ARRAY [0:8, 0:8] STRING
```

When each game starts each index location in the array should be assigned the value "Free".

Write a pseudocode algorithm that assigns the value "Free" to all index locations in the array `Board`.

[3]

7   A business requires that product numbers meet these requirements:

• The product number must begin with the letters "PROD".

• The product number must be 10 characters long.

The product numbers PROD1556DT and PRODa45629 are valid product numbers.

A system is required that will check that product numbers meet the requirements. The system will output the message "Accepted" or "Rejected" depending on whether the product number input meets the rules.

Write the algorithm that will check that product numbers meet the requirements. Use pseudocode or a flowchart.

[6]

8 Rewrite the following pseudocode using a CASE statement.

```
INT Score ← 0
INPUT Score
IF Score > 100
   THEN
      OUTPUT "Excelling"
   ELSE
      IF Score > 80
         THEN
            OUTPUT "Good"

         ELSE
            IF Score > 60
               THEN
                  OUTPUT "Acceptable"
               ELSE
                  OUTPUT "Below expectations"
            ENDIF
      ENDIF
ENDIF
```

[4]

9 A function `convert` is required which will take as a parameter the temperature in Celsius and output the equivalent temperature in Fahrenheit.

The formula to convert from Celsius (C) to Fahrenheit (F) is $F = C * 1.8 + 32$.

Write the pseudocode for the function `convert`.

[2]

10 Programmers make use of variables and constants.

a Explain **one** difference between a variable and a constant.

[2]

Variables and constants are declared using data types.

b Complete the table to show the most appropriate data types for each variable.

Variable	Most appropriate Date Type
`Students` – holds the number of students in a school	
`IDNumber` holds ID numbers. An example is MR145T	
`Weight` – holds the weight of parcels in kilograms	
`Passed` – records whether a person has passed a test	
`Name` – holds the name of students at a school	
`Grade` – holds an examination grade A, B, C, D or E	

[6]

[Total: 8]

CONTINUED

11   A tennis club classifies its members as follows:
   - child if aged less than 10
   - junior if aged 10 to17
   - adult if aged 18 to 59
   - senior if aged 60 or older.

The following is a partially completed flowchart design for a program which would be used to store the classification of members.

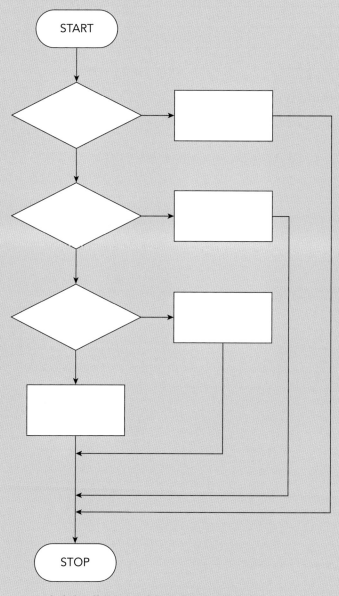

a   Label the diagram with A, B, C and so on.

b   Create a list below which contains each label together with the coding that it represents.

[8]

12 a Define the term **variable**.

[2]

b A school stores data in a computer system regarding students' performance in tests. The following table shows some example data that would be output by the system:

Student Name	Student identifier	Mark	Percentage	Comments	Re-test needed
A Patel	346	60	80	improved	no
W Chi	231	65	87	steady	no
E Brown	458	33	44	disappointing	yes
M Santana	023	42	56	better	no

Choose variable names that you would use if writing this program.

For each variable identify the data type you would use.

[6]

[Total: 8]

13 a i State three reasons why a programmer would choose to use a subroutine. [3]

ii State a difference between a function and a procedure.

[1]

b Consider that a subroutine is to be used to convert a distance in miles into a distance in kilometres.

i Choose a suitable name for the subroutine.

ii Write a pseudocode statement showing how the subroutine would be used if it had been written as a procedure.

iii Write a pseudocode statement showing how the subroutine would be used if it had been written as a function.

[3]

[Total: 7]

14 A program contains a string "oldSTRING" held in a variable named oldString. Using pseudocode or program code write statements that will assign a value to a variable named newString.

a When newString is to be "OLDSTRING".

b When newString is to be "G".

c When newString is to be "o".

d When newString is to be "STRING".

[4]

15 A club is developing a system for dealing with applications for membership. When someone applies to join they are asked for some personal details and the name of someone who will recommend them. The decision as to whether the applicant is accepted is sent to the applicant.

The following structure diagram has been created as a design for the system. You need to provide labels for each box in the diagram.

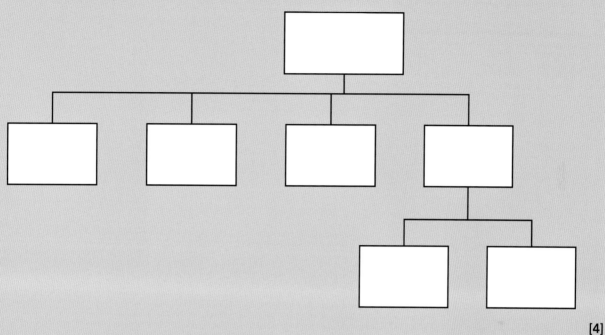

[4]

16 Consider the following fragment of pseudocode:

```
FOR i ← 1 TO n - 1
    swapped ← false
    FOR j ← 0 TO n - 1
        IF list[j] > list[j + 1]
            THEN
                swap(list[j], list[j+1])
                swapped ← true
        ENDIF
    NEXT j
    IF swapped = false
        THEN
            break
    ENDIF
NEXT i
```

a Identify the purpose of this algorithm.

[1]

b Identify and explain the programming constructs that are used.

[5]

[Total: 6]

17 A student was asked to write a program that asks a user to input their first and last names, and their last 5 marathon times in minutes (rounded to the nearest whole minute) and then outputs their average time. The average time should be output in hours and minutes. Here is their algorithm in pseudocode:

```
FUNCTION f(i,j,k,l,m):
    t ← i + j + k + l + m
    RETURN ROUND(t/5)
ENDFUNCTION
INPUT name1
INPUT name2
FOR i ← 1 TO 5
    CASE OF i:
        1: INPUT a
        2: INPUT b
        3: INPUT c
        4: INPUT d
        5: INPUT e
    ENDCASE
NEXT i
ave = f(a,b,c,d,e)
OUTPUT name1 + " " + name2 + " average marathon time:"
OUTPUT (ave DIV 60) + "hrs " + (ave MOD 60) + "mins"
```

a Rewrite the algorithm, keeping its logical flow, but make it easier to read and more manageable.

[6]

b Another programmer tells the student that the algorithm is overly complex and could be produced without the use of the FUNCTION or the CASE statement. Rewrite the algorithm without using FUNCTION or CASE.

[6]

[Total: 12]

18 A simple game app keeps track of the number of lives a player has in a variable called `lives`. Depending on the event that happens, one of the two functions in the code snippet below are called.

```
lives ← 5
gameOver ← FALSE

PROCEDURE loseLife()
    minLives ← 0
    IF lives > minLives
      THEN
          lives ← lives - 1
    ENDIF
    IF lives = 0
      THEN
          gameOver ← TRUE
    ENDIF
ENDPROCEDURE
```

CONTINUED

```
PROCEDURE gainLife()
    maxLives ← 5

    IF lives < maxLives
      THEN
         lives ← lives + 1
    ENDIF
ENDPROCEDURE
```

a   Give the identifiers of all the local variables.

[1]

b   Give the identifiers of all the global variables.

[1]

c   Explain the difference between a local and global variable.

[2]

d   Explain why it is not a good idea to make all variables global.

[2]

[Total: 6]

19 A program needs to read a value from the text file `Score.txt`, increase it by 1 and then store the new value back in the text file. The program must also check that the new score has not reached 10. If the score is 10 or above then the program calls the `GameOver()` procedure.

Write an algorithm, using pseudocode or program code, to perform this part of the larger program.

[6]

20 A program is required that creates usernames and passwords from users' first and last names. First the program must ask a user to input their `firstname` and then their `lastname`. It then creates a username from the first two letters of the `firstname` and the last five letters of the `lastname`. The `username` is entirely lower case. The program then creates a `password` that is made by creating a random six figure number that does not start with `0`. Finally it outputs the `username` and `password` for this user.

Assumptions:

*   Ignore possible duplicate usernames.
*   Users' first and last names only contain letters (no hyphens or apostrophes or accents).
*   Users' first and last names may contain a mixture of upper case and lower case letters.
*   Users' first and last names always contain more than 3 letters and 5 letters respectively.
*   For the purpose of this question, there is no storage of the username and password produced.

Write an algorithm, using pseudocode or program code, to perform this part of the larger program.

[6]

21 A simple computer game currently stores a map of rooms in a 10 × 10 grid in ten arrays like this:

```
row0[0:9] OF String
row1[0:9] OF String
row2[0:9] OF String
etc.
```

a   Why would it be better to store the map data in a single 2D array?

[3]

CONTINUED

b Provide the declaration in pseudocode for a 2D array, map, that can be used to store all the information in the ten 1D arrays currently used.

[1]

c A reference to an image is stored in map[2][2], for example, 'hall1.png'. Stored in map[4][4] is a reference to another image. During the game these two image references need to be swapped around. Write the pseudocode that would swap the two image references in the map array. In your answer you must assume that the current images being shown in the 'rooms' have to be found, by your program, from the array.

[3]

[Total: 7]

22 A database contains a table, Bats, that stores data about some bats at a zoo. Below is the table showing the data stored (all weights are in grams and lengths in millimetres):

BatID	Name	Type	Wingspan	Weight	Length
1	Omar	Pipistrelle	120	18	85
2	Sally	Long-eared	245	7	47
3	Sergei	Fruit	1010	890	25
4	Julia	Vampire	203	56	90
5	Rana	Horseshoe	210	7	41
6	Jerry	Mouse-tailed	110	10	70
7	Sheila	Pipistrelle	120	19	85
8	Suzie	Fruit	990	950	24

a Why is a BatID field included in the database?

[2]

b What is the appropriate data type for the data held in the Type field?

[1]

c What data will be returned by the following SQL queries (show in table with field headings):

i
```
SELECT Name FROM Bats
WHERE Type = 'Pipistrelle'
ORDER BY Name ASC;
```

[1]

ii
```
SELECT * FROM Bats
WHERE Type = 'Pipistrelle';
```

[1]

d Write the SQL query that will:

i Return the number of Pipistrelle bats in the database.

[2]

ii Return all the Names of the bats (in alphabetical order) that weigh under 20 g.

[3]

[Total: 10]

> Appendix 1

Turtle reference

This provides the most important turtle commands that can be used after importing the Python turtle module like this:

```
from turtle import *
```

Command	Arguments	Example
forward()	Distance in pixels	forward(50)
back()	Distance in pixels	back(50)
right()	Angle in degrees	right(90)
left()	Angle in degrees	left(90)
home()	None required (turtle goes to coordinates (0,0))	
penup()	None required	
pendown()	None required	
speed()	10 = fast, 6 = normal, 1 = slow 0 = as fast as possible	speed(6)
pensize()	Line width in pixels	pensize(10)
pencolor()	Common colours	pencolor('red')
shape()	arrow, turtle, circle, square, triangle, classic	shape('turtle')
circle()	Radius in pixels extent = angle of circle to draw steps = lines used to make the circle (can make regular polygons)	# Draw circle circle(50) # Draw pentagon circle(50, steps=5)
fillcolor()	Common colours	fillcolor('violet')
begin_fill()	None required (creates a start point to fill a shape)	
end_fill()	None required (creates a stop point when filling a shape)	
hideturtle()	None required	
showturtle()	None required	
color()	Common colours (turtle colour)	color('brown')
goto()	x and y coordinates from the origin in pixels	goto(50,60)
done()	None required (tells Python to stop waiting for turtle commands)	

Table Appendix 1: Useful turtle commands

> Appendix 2
Tkinter
reference

> **Note:** Producing GUI based applications is optional. It goes beyond what you need to know for the syllabuses.

This appendix is intended as a quick reminder of the code required to add tkinter widgets to your GUIs. It is not a syllabus requirement to build GUI applications. However, it is also not very difficult to do.

An empty window

```
from tkinter import *
# Create the main tkinter window
window = Tk()
window.title('My Application')

# Add widgets here

# Enter the main event loop
window.mainloop()
```

A frame

```
frame1 = Frame(window,height=20, width=100, bg='green')
frame1.grid(row=0, column=0)
```

A label

```
my_label = Label(window, width=25, height=1, text='My Label')
my_label.grid(row=0, column=0)
```

An image label

```
# Import gif image from images folder in the same folder as the script
my_image = PhotoImage(file='images/my_image.gif')

# Add image to label widget
my_label = Label(window, image='my_image')
my_label.grid(row=0, column=0)
```

An empty label as a spacer

```
my_label = Label(window, width=20, height=1, text='')
my_label.grid(row=0, column=0)
```

A button

```
my_button = Button(window, text='Submit', width=10, command=click_function)
my_button.grid(row=1, column=0)
```

A text entry box

```
# Create and place a text entry box
my_text_entry_box = Entry(window, width=15)
my_text_entry_box.grid(row=0, column=0)

# Get string from text entry box
user_text = my_text_entry_box.get()

# Clear the text entry box
my_text_entry_box.delete(0, END)
```

A text box

```
my_text_box = Text(window, width=15, height=5)
my_text_box.grid(row=0, column=0)
```

A scrolling text box

```
my_text_box = ScrolledText(window, width=15, height=5, wrap=WORD)
my_text_box.grid(row=0, column=0)
```

A drop-down menu (with integers)

```
# Create a tuple of menu items
options = (1,2,3)

# Create a tkinter string variable object for the radiobuttons
my_variable_object = IntVar()  # access the value with my_variable_object.get()
my_variable_object.set('choose:')
my_dropdown = OptionMenu(window, my_variable_object, *options)
my_dropdown.grid(row=0, column=0)
```

Radio button menu (with strings)

```
# Create a tkinter string variable object for the radiobuttons
gender = StringVar()  # access the value with my_variable.get()

# Add two radiobutton widgets
radio1 = Radiobutton(window, text='Female', variable=gender, value='female')
radio1.grid(row=0, column=0)
radio1.select()  # pre-selects this radio button
radio2 = Radiobutton(window, text='Male', variable=gender, value='male')
radio2.grid(row=1, column=0)
```

Checkboxes

```
# Create three checkboxes
# var1, var2 and var3 return either 0 (unselected) or 1 (selected)
var1 = IntVar()   # access the value with var1.get()
checkbox1 = Checkbutton(window, text='Python', variable=var1)
checkbox1.grid(row=0, column=0)
var2 = IntVar()   # access the value with var2.get()
checkbox2 = Checkbutton(window, text='Visual Basic', variable=var2)
checkbox2.grid(row=1, column=0)
var3 = IntVar()   # access the value with var3.get()
checkbox3 = Checkbutton(window, text='Java', variable=var3)
checkbox3.grid(row=2, column=0)
```

> Glossary

abstraction: a computational thinking skill that involves spotting key information in a problem and hiding unnecessary information. This is most often done by programmers when details of an algorithm are abstracted into a subroutine.

algorithm: a process, instructions or set of rules to be followed during the execution of a program.

alpha testing: early testing that takes place when a system has had all of its main features added for the first time.

arguments: when a program calls a subroutine, it may need to pass some values to it. Parameters are the names of the variables. Arguments are the actual values passed.

array: a data structure that can hold a set of data items of the same data type under a single identifier.

array index: a number that refers to an item in an array.

assignment: passing a value, such as some text or a number, to a named variable.

average: the mean of a set of values, the total divided by the quantity.

beta testing: formal testing by users once the system has been completed and passed through a company's internal testing regime.

Boolean: describes an operator, function or variable that only deals with True or False.

Boolean operators: The operators AND, OR and NOT allow a program to make a decision based on more than one condition.

built-in: when programming, we can write our own commands. Python comes with some ready-made commands and modules. The `print()` function is a built-in function and turtle is an example of a built-in module.

call: to activate a subroutine. To do this, you specify the subroutine's name and, optionally, parameters.

CASE statements: a simple method of providing multiple paths through the code based on a single variable or user input.

cast: the process of changing the data type of a given variable into another data type. For example, a variable that holds the string value '2' could be cast into an integer variable storing the value 2.

commenting: adding human readable notes to a program. The comments are intended to help explain how the code works. Comments are ignored by the computer when the code is executed. In pseudocode, comments are preceded with two forward slashes // and in Python by a hash symbol #.

condition-controlled loops: types of iteration where the repetition of the loop is determined by conditions. The amount of times the loop will be executed is unknown.

constant: a named memory location used to store a value; the value can be used but not changed during program execution. (However, in Python, we use normal variables but indicate that the value of the data should not be changed by giving it a name in all capitals, e.g. PI = 3.14.)

construct: a method of controlling the order in which the statements in an algorithm are executed.

container data type: a data type that can contain more than one data item (e.g. arrays and lists).

counting: a standard method of solution, used in programs, that adds one for every item in a set of values to find out how many there are.

data integrity: the correctness of data during and after processing.

data type: a specification of the kind of value that a variable will store.

debugging: a general term for systematically searching for problems in programs that are not working properly and fixing them.

declarative language: a programming language where precise instructions are written in a program but the language looks after how this is achieved.

declaring variables: setting up a variable or constant. It is important to declare or initialise global variables.

decomposition: a computational thinking skill that involves thinking about large tasks and breaking them down into smaller tasks.

diagnostics: the systematic process of trying to diagnose what is wrong with a program.

divide-by-zero errors: divide-by-zero errors occur when a number is being divided by a variable that has the value zero. A divide-by-zero error will stop the program running. (Another example of runtime errors.)

double entry: a verification technique where the same data has to be entered twice and the computer checks that both entries are the same before accepting the data as valid.

event-driven system: an application that runs in an infinite loop and can react to events that occur while the program is running such as user input or a sprite colliding with the wall of a window.

execute: another word for run. Programmers tend to prefer to talk about a program executing rather than running, but they mean the same thing.

field: a column of data held in a database table.

flowchart: a graphical representation of the sequence and logic of a program.

FOR Loop: a type of iteration that will repeat a section of code a known number of times. Also known as a count-controlled loop.

function: a subroutine that can receive multiple parameters and returns a single value. A function always returns a value through its identifier.

global variable: a variable that can be accessed from any routine within the program.

graphical user interface (GUI): an interface that includes graphical elements, such as windows, icons and buttons.

identifier: the unique name given to elements of a program, such as variables, constants and functions. An identifier can then be used to represent the named element elsewhere in the program.

IDLE: the IDE provided when Python is installed.

IF statements: a statement that allows a program to follow or ignore a sequence of code depending on a Boolean condition.

infinite loop: a type of iteration that has no termination condition and so goes on forever. This is sometimes created accidently by an error in a loop condition. There are also genuine uses, such as when an app has to always be listening for button presses.

initialising variables: giving a variable a start (initial) value when it is first declared.

input: data that is required by a program to complete the required task. The data can be obtained from the user, a file or database, a device or another program.

Integrated Development Environment (IDE): software that helps programmers to design, create and test program code.

interactive mode: when writing and running code in the Python shell window, interactive mode allows us to try out snippets of code without saving.

iteration: code repeats a certain sequence a number of times depending on certain conditions.

list: a container data type that is available to Python programmers that can be used to implement algorithms requiring arrays.

local variable: a variable that can only be accessed in the code element in which it is declared.

logical errors: result in code that runs but produces unexpected results.

logical operators: allow programs to make a decision when comparing to conditions. They are sometimes called comparison operators. They include <, >, <=, >= and !=.

loop counter: a variable that is used within a FOR loop to keep a record of the number of times the loop has been repeated. The loop counter normally increases by 1 each time the loop is executed.

loosely typed: programming languages where the programmer does not have to declare the variable type when initialising or declaring variables.

main event loop: a loop that iterates the whole time the program is running. Its main job is to 'listen' for user input and to call subroutines to handle the input.

maximum: the largest item in a set of data.

minimum: the smallest item in a set of data.

nested IF: an IF statement with the ability for additional conditions to be checked once earlier conditions have determined a path.

one-dimensional array: a linear array with a single index set. Contains one row of data with multiple elements; each element is identified by a unique index number.

output: textual, visual or audio data that is produced by a program. The output can be sent to an output device, stored in a file or database or displayed to a user.

overflow errors: overflow errors occur when the data passed to a variable is too large to be held by the data type selected. (Another example of runtime errors.)

parameters: data or values that are passed to, or received from, a subroutine.

pass: a subroutine may require some values to compute with. When this is the case we say the values are passed to the subroutine.

primary key: a field in a database table that holds unique values that can be used to identify each record in the table.

procedure: a subroutine that can receive and return multiple parameters. It may or may not return a value. If values are returned, they are returned via parameters.

process: a part of a program where the input data is used to complete the required task.

pseudocode: a way of unambiguously representing the sequence and logic of a program using both natural language and code-like statements.

Python shell: a window that allows Python programmers to write and run code a line at a time without having to save the code in a file. It is also where users can provide input and where output is sent.

query: a question asked of a database when using the SQL language.

record: a row of data held in a database table.

refactoring: the process of pulling out repeating lines of code into subroutines and loops.

REPEAT...UNTIL loop: a type of iteration that will repeat a sequence of code until a certain condition is met. The code within the loop will always be executed at least once.

runtime errors: problems with the code that only become evident when the program is run, for example, attempting to divide by zero.

script mode: Python scripts are written in a text editor or IDE and saved with the .py extension. Script mode enables programmers to write longer programs that can be edited or run at any time in the future.

selection: code follows a different sequence based on what condition is chosen.

sequence: code is executed in the order it is written.

slicing: a facility in Python that allows a programmer to select a specified portion of a string.

SQL: Structured Query Language is a programming language used to manage and search databases.

standard methods of solution: methods of solving problems that occur commonly in computer programs, e.g. linear search, bubble sort, totalling, counting, finding maximum, minimum and average values.

string: a data type that is used to hold a portion of text. As well as letters, a string can also include numbers, spaces and punctuation.

structure diagrams: a method of expressing a system as a series of subsystems using a diagram.

subroutine: subroutines provide an independent section of code that can be called from another routine while the program is running. In this way, subroutines can be used to perform common tasks within a program.

substring: a portion of a string.

syntax: the specific words, symbols and constructs defined for use by a particular language. It is the equivalent of grammar in creative writing.

syntax errors: mistakes made in the code equivalent to spelling and punctuation mistakes in English.

tkinter: a module that is provided as part of the standard library in Python. It provides tools to help the programmer build applications that have buttons, textboxes, etc.

top-down design: a way of designing a computer program by breaking down the problem into smaller problems (subsystems) until it is sufficiently defined to allow it to be understood and programmed. This is sometimes known as step-wise refinement.

totalling: a standard method of solution, used in programs, that adds up multiple values to find the total.

trace tables: a way to test and find bugs in programs. A table is constructed to keep track of the values held in variables as a program is stepped through line by line.

two-dimensional array: an array with two index sets. Contains multiple rows of data with multiple columns. Each individual element identified by a combination of both row and column index.

validation: the process of programming a system to automatically check that data satisfies a set of specified input criteria; for example, passwords must be longer than six characters.

variable: a memory location used to store a value; the value of the data can be changed during program execution.

verification: a process that confirms the integrity of data as it is input into the system or when it is transferred between different parts of a system; for example, a CAPTCHA image used to prove data is being entered by a human.

visual check: a verification technique where previously entered data is presented back to either the data entry person, or someone else, to check and confirm it is correct.

WHILE loop: a loop construct with a condition at the start of the loop to determine whether iteration should continue.

widget: interface items such as buttons and text boxes that can be used to build GUIs.

> Acknowledgements

The authors and publishers acknowledge the following sources of copyright material and are grateful for the permissions granted. While every effort has been made, it has not always been possible to identify the sources of all the material used, or to trace all copyright holders. If any omissions are brought to our notice, we will be happy to include the appropriate acknowledgements on reprinting.

Python is a registered trademark of the Python Software Foundation.

Thanks to the following for permission to reproduce images:

Cover Nerthuz/Getty Images

Inside Chapter 1 John Lund/Getty Images, Fig 1.07 John Howard/Science Photo Library, Chapter 2 Andriy Onufriyenko/Getty Images, Chapter 3 Yuichiro Chino/Getty Images, Chapter 4 Andrew Brookes/Getty Images, Chapter 5 AniGraphics/Getty Images, Chapter 6 zf L/Getty Images, izusek/Getty Images; Chapter 7 schulz/Getty Images, Chapter 8 KTSDESIGN/SCIENCE PHOTO LIBRARY via Getty Images, Chapter 9 Nikada/Getty Images, Chapter 10 Rizky Panuntun/Getty Images, Chapter 11 Yuichiro Chino/Getty Images, Chapter 12 Nora Carol Photography/Getty Images, Chapter 13 Yuichiro Chino/Getty Images, Westend61/Getty Images, Chapter 14 filo/Getty Images, Chapter 15 MR.Cole_Photographer Getty Images, Appendix 1 SEAN GLADWELL/Getty Images, Appendix 2 angelhell/Getty Images